Performance Research Associates

Delivering Knock Your Socks Off Service

20th Anniversary Edition

Artwork by John Bush
Edited by Ann Thomas and Jill Applegate

© Performance Research Associates, 2012

American Management Association

New York • Atlanta • Brussels • Boston • Chicago • Mexico City • San Francisco

Bulk discounts available. For details visit:
www.amacombooks.org/go/specialsales

Or contact special sales:
Phone: 800-250-5308
Email: specialsls@amanet.org
View all the AMACOM titles at:
www.amacombooks.org

This publication is designed to provide accurate and authoritative information in regard to the subject matter covered. It is sold with the understanding that the publisher is not engaged in rendering legal, accounting, or other professional service. If legal advice or other expert assistance is required, the services of a competent professional person should be sought.

Library of Congress Cataloging-in-Publication Data

Performance Research Associates, Inc.
  Delivering knock your socks off service / Performance Research Associates. — 5th updated and rev. ed.
     p. cm.
"20th anniversary edition."
Includes bibliographical references and index.
ISBN-13: 978-0-8144-1755-3
ISBN-10: 0-8144-1755-8
1. Customer services. I. Title.
HF5415.5.A53 2012
658.8'12—dc22

                                                                    2011014619

About AMA
American Management Association (www.amanet.org) is a world leader in talent development, advancing the skills of individuals to drive business success. Our mission is to support the goals of individuals and organizations through a complete range of products and services, including classroom and virtual seminars, webcasts, webinars, podcasts, conferences, corporate and government solutions, business books and research. AMA's approach to improving performance combines experiential learning—learning through doing—with opportunities for ongoing professional growth at every step of one's career journey.

Printing number

20 19 18 17 16 15

Contents

Foreword

When I thought about writing a forward for the 20th anniversary edition of *Delivering Knock Your Socks Off Service*, I didn't know what I could possibly say that hadn't been covered already. When Ron first suggested the idea that service mattered it seemed like a blinding flash of the obvious—treat customers well, be successful, we all have a good day. As we traveled together, went to restaurants, got the cars repaired and the dry cleaning done, and consumed all manner of services great and small it became apparent that this was not obvious at all.

Ever the optimist, though, Ron persevered. He truly believed that people really did want to provide excellent service and treat each other well; they just needed to know how. In the ensuing years, he enlisted wonderful coauthors in writing a series of books to show the way.

With Chip Bell he helped managers understand how to train, support, and motivate the people on the front lines of great service every day with *Managing Knock Your Socks Off Service*. Knowing that things don't always go as planned, he and Chip wrote *Knock Your Socks Off Service Recovery*, a book discussing what to do when things go completely awry.

With Kristin Anderson, Ron helped managers learn to coach and develop their people, and provided answers for even the most challenging and, frankly, wacky questions customers can ask. *Coaching Knock Your Socks Off Service* and *Knock Your Socks Off Answers* continued Ron's quest for and belief that wonderful service experiences are always possible.

While all this was good, Ron and Tom Connellan recognized that high quality service, delivered consistently over time was the key to long-term customer delight and retention. They collaborated on *Sustaining Knock Your Socks Off Service*, providing businesses with ways to build outstanding service into the fabric of their cultures.

With *101 Activities for Delivering Knock Your Socks Off Service,* Ann Thomas and Jill Applegate have continued to reinforce Ron's belief that people want to deliver great service and that great service is possible and profitable; they just need some help sometimes.

Here we are 20 years later. This 20th anniversary edition of *DKYSOS* celebrates Ron's legacy of service, optimism, faith in others' good intentions, and belief that we can all have and deliver Knock Your Socks Off Service.

Susan Zemke

Our Thanks

Wow! Who would have ever thought that what began as a simple, fun, easy-to-read front-line customer service book in 1990 would still have such an impact 20 years later! Yet here we are penning this special anniversary edition. And, as is the case with every book Performance Research Associates has undertaken, it's never done alone!

On this unique occasion, we want to pay special attention to those who are no longer with us. Without question, none of this would have been possible without the extraordinary vision of Ron Zemke. The "father" of the Knock Your Socks Off Service series, Ron's presence is still felt in each and every one of the book's pages. What a tribute to Ron this 20th anniversary edition is—without him, there would never have been a chapter written, let alone a 9-book series and multiple revisions. We love you, Ron and still miss you every day.

John Bush made such a huge contribution to this series. Like Ron, we lost John far too soon. His illustrations still make us laugh all these years later, and we continue to marvel at his creativity and the ease with which he could draw the perfect cartoon. He was sometimes subtle and sometimes obvious—but he was always on target and always left us wanting more. We miss not having any new art to share in this edition but are grateful that the images that John left with us will live on.

A very special thank you to Susan Zemke for writing the foreword for this edition. We knew there was only one person who could do it justice, and Susan definitely lived up to the challenge. We are grateful for her friendship, her ongoing support, and her commitment to ensuring that Ron's work and legacy continues as an inspiration to others.

Ellen Kadin and the team at AMACOM have been our partners in this endeavor for more than two decades. It is a trusted relationship that we value tremendously. Thank you for your ongoing support, Ellen.

Much has changed over the past two decades. The Internet was barely a blip on the radar in 1991. We listened to music on a CD player, never on a phone. Gas prices were substantially lower, and Google wasn't even a word, let alone a verb. But a few things haven't changed. Customers are still the reason we go to work every day. And customers still deserve to receive outstanding service, day in and day out! Our hope is the same now as it was in 1991: That we will continue to provide you the tips, tools, and techniques you need to knock the socks off your customer at each and every encounter!

Here's to 20 more years!

Performance Research Associates
February 2011

Preface

What You Do Is Critically Important

"It's not enough to merely satisfy the customer; customers must be 'delighted'— surprised by having their needs not just met, but exceeded."
—A. Blanton Godfrey

Serving customers. The two words cover so much. Answering questions. Solving problems. Untangling corporate logjams. Fixing what's broken and finding what's lost. Soothing the irate and reassuring the timid. And time after time, performing the business equivalent of pulling a rabbit out of a hat.

Not too long ago, working in customer service was just about as thankless a job as a person could find. Sales? That was a job with a future. Marketing? Now there was a title with some prestige. Digital marketing? Wow, the wave of the future. Advertising? What mystique! Web page design—really cool! But customer service? Backwater. A burden. A career path to nowhere. Fellow employees looked down their noses at "those people who deal with whining customers." And customers—well, they mostly seemed to see customer service as a title for not very bright people who woke up most mornings, looked in the mirror, grinned wide, and said to their reflections, "This is going to be a fun day. I'm going to go down there and annoy the first 217 people I talk to." And then did just that. Not exactly positive images.

In the late 1990s, about the time of the dot.com debacle, professional business watchers began to re-learn something important. They discovered that organizations that had dedicated themselves to working hard at giving their customers superior service were producing better financial results. These organizations grew faster and were more profitable than the organizations that were still working as hard as they could to give their customers as little as possible, whether online, over the phone, or face-to-face. Now, in the second decade of the new millennium, it's not just about focusing on customers, it's about creating loyal ones. That's where the real money is.

In short, companies that emphasize total customer service make more money and keep customers longer than companies that don't.

Researchers also started to notice that highly successful service organizations had lower marketing costs, fewer upset and complaining customers, and more repeat business—customers were "voting with their feet" and beating a path back to the doors of the companies that served them well. What's more, good service had internal rewards: Employee turnover and absenteeism were lower and morale and job satisfaction higher in these same organizations. Companies that asked employees to make customers happy had happier employees.

Almost overnight, being customer-focused, understanding and meeting customer needs, and coddling customers with Tender Loving Care became a critical organizational goal. And received spotlight attention. Books were written. Banners hung. And speeches made—all trumpeting the importance of customer service. A revolution in the way customer service was viewed and valued began—and continues to this day.

In the two decades since the start of the latest service revolution, we've all learned a lot about what it takes to create and sustain a service advantage. As the world grows ever smaller, we've learned that good service requires a new sensitivity to the cultural differences and varied service expectations of customers we serve around the globe. As Baby Boomers, Generation Xers, and Millennials continue to collide in the workplace, we've learned that each generation has distinct service preferences that we need to account for in how we plan or deliver service. And for all we've learned, for all that has been written and said, the most important part of creating a "service advantage" is still... you.

What you do is important. What you do is work—hard work. Answering questions. Solving problems. Untangling corporate logjams. Fixing what's broken and finding what's lost. Soothing the irate and reassuring the timid. Matching people you do business with with just the right products and services, and helping them enjoy and get the most out of those purchases.

Twenty years ago, Ron and Kristin penned the original *Delivering Knock Your Socks Off Service* to share with you what we had learned about quality customer care during fifteen years of watching and working with thousands of customer-oriented customer service professionals. People just like you who provide great service over and over and over again; true Knock Your Socks Off Service pros who make their customers' lives and jobs simpler instead of more difficult, more interesting and less boring—and who have a heck of a good time doing it, too.

In the ensuing two decades we have had the opportunity to work with thousands of customer service professionals worldwide. And we have learned even more about the fine art of delivering world class customer care. We have taken those lessons in hand and to heart, and we present here for your consideration the *Delivering Knock Your Socks Off Service: 20th Anniversary Edition.* You'll notice something new in the back matter of this edition: We have included a cross reference feature that ties back to our book, *101 Activities for Knock Your Socks Off Service*. The recommended activities are tied to specific chapters of this book as an additional resource.

Whether you are new to customer service or an old pro, we think there is something here for you. What you do is more important to your organization than ever before. If this book helps you to do it even a little bit better, your thanks should go not to us, but to the thousands of pros who served as our teachers and mentors. And if you find the journey through these pages not only helpful but enjoyable, then we'll have met *our* customer service goal.

Performance Research Associates
Minneapolis, MN
February 2011

I

The Fundamental Principles of Knock Your Socks Off Service

Delivering Knock Your Socks Off Service—the kind of service that makes a positive, lasting impression on your customers—takes more than simple courtesy. Much more.

The first fundamental is understanding what good service is from your customer's point of view. What you do, how you do it, knowing how well it must be done, and doing it again and again—those are fundamental as well.

Delivering Knock Your Socks Off Service means creating a positive, memorable experience for every customer. It means exceeding expectations and satisfying needs—and in such a way that you're seen as easy to do business with. It means looking for opportunities to wow and delight your customer in unique and unexpected ways.

The customer who experiences all that will be your customer again and again. When you deliver Knock Your Socks Off Service, everybody wins: Your customer, your company, and *you*.

1

The Only Unbreakable Rule:

To the Customer, *You* Are the Company

"Customer relations is an integral part of your job—not an extension of it."

—William B. Martin

Quality Customer Service

Customers don't distinguish between you and the organization you work for. Nor should they. To your customer's way of thinking, you *are* the company.

Customers don't know how things get done behind doors or from the ends of the fingers that send company Tweets, Facebook posts, or e-mails. They don't know your areas of responsibility, your job description, or what you personally can and cannot do for them. And they don't care. To customers, those things are *your* business, not theirs.

Their attitude and focus is clear and straightforward: "Help me with this purchase, please." "Serve me my meal."

"Solve my problem." "Process my order, *now*." Whether customers' feelings about the company are good or bad often relates directly to their experience with you and the way you help them meet their needs.

Each interaction between a customer and a service professional is one moment in the chain of the customer's experience. If you're a service person, and you get it wrong at your link in the chain, you are very likely erasing from the customer's mind all the memories of good treatment he or she may have had up to that moment. But if you get it right, you have a chance to undo all the wrongs that may have happened before the customer got to you. And, in today's world, the faster you do it, the happier they are.

Consider this small example from a trip to Walt Disney World—the land where magical service abounds! A friend of ours was there recently, enjoying a hot, summer day at the Magic Kingdom. After waiting in line for about 20 minutes for an ice cream cone, she started off down Main Street USA, licking intently. She glanced away for a second, and when she looked back, found herself staring dumbfounded at an empty cone! What had happened? An uninvited sea gull had swooped down and scooped the ice cream right out of the cone. She was stunned, but continued her walk down Main Street more than a little miffed at the situation. Seconds later, a young man carrying a broom and dust pan, approached her: "Excuse me, Ma'am, I saw that bird dive at your ice cream. Unfortunately, I see that fairly frequently. Disney's sea gulls pretty much know no fear. May I escort you back to get you another cone? That was cookies and cream, wasn't it?" Our friend was thunderstruck. What could have been a negative moment turned full circle and is now a favorite Disney World memory; one she loves to share with others.

Just like that Disney employee, you can make or break the chain of great service and memorable experiences. Is it fair that so much can depend upon you? Nope. But fair has nothing to do with it.

When your job involves serving customers and dealing with the public, how good a job you do with and for them—for the nice and the nasty, the smart and the dumb, the people you'd like to take home to mother, and those you really wish had never been born—determines how successful your company will be. In short:

> You Are The Company.

> **TIP:** Use *I* instead of *they* or *we*. To a customer, the company begins and ends with you. Using *I* shows that you understand and accept that: "*I'm* sorry you had to look so long to find the dress department. May *I* help you find anything else?"

Being the Company: It's Everything You Do

Some of the things you do to provide Knock Your Socks Off Service are relatively simple and easy, such as choosing your language carefully.

Other actions you take are more complex. Customers expect you to make the organization work for them. They expect you to understand the big picture and to be able to answer their questions, solve their problems, and refer them to just the right people for just the right things.

> **TIP:** Saying "the *policy* is. . . ." or "*they* won't allow . . . ." tells customers you are just a clerk. If that's the way you feel, you won't ever be able to help them—and could easily be replaced by a machine or walked on like so much carpet. Verbally separating yourself from the company in the customer's mind can take you off the hot seat with unhappy customers, but it plants a seed of doubt in the customer's mind. It says "you may not be able to trust me to help you."

What your customers want and need is changing constantly. So is your company, and so are you. How can you possibly keep up? Let the following three questions guide your

personal-service efforts. Don't just ask them once. Ask them all the time. Use the information they provide to choose actions that will Knock the Socks Off your customers.

1. *What do my customers want from me, and from my company?* Think about what your customers *need* and what your customers *expect*. If you don't know—ask around. The seasoned senior associates will have a pretty good idea.

2. *How do support areas—for example, billing or shipping—work to serve my customers?* Consider your role in helping the different areas of your company work in harmony for your customer. Who do you need in your corner to help you help your customers?

3. *What are the details—little things—that make a big difference in my customers' satisfaction?* Knock Your Socks Off Service means paying attention to what's important in your customers' eyes. Do you know what counts for your customers?

Being the company to your customers is what makes the work you do both challenging and rewarding. In your one-on-

one interaction with customers, the once vague, impersonal company takes on shape and substance. In your hands is the power to make that contact magical and memorable. In your hands is the power to keep customers coming back.

From this moment forward, make this your pledge:

2

Know What Knock Your Socks Off Service Is

"Customers perceive service in their own unique, idiosyncratic, emotional, irrational, end-of-the-day, and totally human terms. Perception is all there is!"

—Tom Peters
Management guru

Customers are demanding. And they have every right to be. Today's customers have more options—and less time—than ever before. If your organization doesn't offer what they want or need, if you don't interact with them in a manner that meets or exceeds their expectations, or if you aren't quick about it, they will just walk on down the street—or let their fingers surf the 'net—and do business with one of your competitors.

And if you don't have customers, you don't have a job!

Researchers consistently find that it costs *five times more* to attract a new customer than it does to keep one you already have. But many businesses think only of making the sale instead of developing long-term customer relationships. Even more disturbing, researchers also find that at any given time, as many as *one customer in four* is dissatisfied enough to start doing business with someone else—if he or she can find someone else who promises to do the same thing that you do but in a slightly more satisfying way. That's as many as twenty-five out of every one hundred people your organization does business with.

8

Most disturbing of all is the finding that *only one* of those twenty-five dissatisfied customers will ever tell you that he or she is dissatisfied. Today's customers are more likely to put a review on a web site (Yelp, City Search, Twitter, Facebook) that could have significant impact on your business. In fact, you've probably noticed from your own experience how rare it is to deal with customers who can do a really good job of telling you what they want. More often, they just expect you to know—and are disappointed when you don't.

That's why companies spend a lot of time and money these days observing customers as they shop—trolling the Internet, monitoring web sites, talking to them on the phone, and meeting them face-to-face. Like miners working a claim for the gold they know is there, today's businesses collect and sort customer comments, looking for the complaints and the compliments that provide clues about what people want today—and how their needs may change tomorrow.

As a customer service professional, you frequently draw on the knowledge your company has acquired about customers. But you have another, equally important source of information: your own day-to-day contact with your customers. From personal experience, you know quite a lot about what your customers want: which actions meet their expectations, which exceed them—and which disappoint them. You are the "listening post" for your organization.

That's your own special edge, the foundation on which to build your own unique way of providing Knock Your Socks Off Service.

Getting Yourself Organized: The RATER Factors

It's helpful to have a framework that captures the multiple service factors that determine the quality of a customer's experience with your company. The framework we like a lot was invented by Texas A&M researcher Dr. Leonard Berry and his colleagues at Texas A&M University. They have found that customers evaluate service quality on five factors:

1. *Reliability.* The ability to provide what was promised, dependably and accurately.
2. *Assurance.* The knowledge and courtesy you show to customers and your ability to convey trust, competence, and confidence.
3. *Tangibles.* The physical facilities and equipment and your own (and others') appearance.
4. *Empathy.* The degree of caring and individual attention you show customers.
5. *Responsiveness.* The willingness to help customers promptly.

Chances are, almost everything you do to and for your customers falls into one of these categories. Consider these common examples:

- When you fulfill a customer order on time, you show *reliability*.
- When you smile and tell a customer, "I can help you with that"—and do—you build *assurance*.
- When you take the time to make yourself and your work area presentable, you are paying attention to the *tangibles*.
- When you are sensitive to an individual customer's needs when solving a problem, you show *empathy*.
- When you notice a customer puzzling over a product and offer help and information, you show *responsiveness*.

All five factors are important to your customers. In the next five chapters, we'll look at each of these pieces of the customer service puzzle in more detail to see how they combine to create people-pleasing Knock Your Socks Off Service.

TIP: Combining the first letter of each factor— **R**eliability, **A**ssurance, **T**angibles, **E**mpathy, **R**esponsiveness, spells the word RATER. It is a handy way to remember these important attributes. Try organizing what you know about clients using RATER. Example: In Mr. Smith's file, next to Responsiveness, you could have a note that reminds you of his responsiveness preferences. Something like "Customer is sensitive to call backs. Return all his calls ASAP."

"Customer expectations of service organizations are loud and clear: look good, be responsive, be reassuring through courtesy and competence, be empathetic but, most of all, be reliable. Do what you said you would do. Keep the service promise."

—Dr. Leonard Berry
Researcher, Texas A&M University

3

Knock Your Socks Off Service Is:

Reliable

"Undertake not what you cannot perform and be careful to keep your promise."

—George Washington

As commander-in-chief of the Continental forces in the American Revolution, George Washington was well aware that the lives of thousands of men and the fate of an emerging nation rested on his ability to know what could and could not be accomplished. He had to deliver on his commitments. There was no room for misjudging the situation.

As a service professional, you are part of another kind of revolution: the service revolution. And while lives are seldom on the line, a little piece of the future of your company is—every time you face a customer. That's where reliability comes in.

The Service Promise

Reliability means keeping the service promise—doing what you say you will do for the customer. To the customer, the service promise has three distinct parts: Organizational commitments, common expectations, and personal promises.

12

- *Organizational Commitments:* Organizations make direct promises to customers through advertising, on their Web sites and marketing materials, in company correspondence and contracts, and in service guarantees and policies published for everyone to see. In addition to these, customers will hold the company to indirect commitments—promises that customers believe are implied in the way the company talks about itself, its products, and its services. Or customers may hold organizations to commitments that they believe are "standard" for the industry.

Consider customer expectations about overnight delivery services. FedEx Corporation, an international overnight delivery service, promises and provides moment-by-moment package tracing. If you want to confirm that your package will arrive on time, simply tap into FedEx's computer tracking system to learn that your package is in a truck on the corner of Maple and Vine, expected to reach its destination within 15 minutes. Other shipping companies should not be surprised when customers demand, "What do you mean you can't tell me exactly where my package is? You're in the overnight shipping business so you have to be able to do that!" Fair or not, FedEx set a standard others are being held to. What standards has your competition set for you?

- *Common Expectations:* Your customers bring additional expectations with them to every service transaction. Based on their past experiences with you and with other service providers, customers make assumptions about what you can and can't do for them. Failing to meet a customer expectation, whether you knew about it or not—even whether you helped to shape it or not—has the same impact as breaking any other promise.

For example, many restaurants routinely post a sign warning that they "cannot be responsible for items left in the cloak room." However, when customers hand their items directly to an attendant, most assume that the belongings will be guarded. Having a staffed coat check rather than an isolated coat rack creates an expectation of security, even if there is a clear warning to the contrary.

- **Personal Promises:** The majority of customer service promises come from you. These are the promises you make when you tell a customer, "I'll get right back to you with that information" or "You should expect to receive that package in two weeks," or "I understand the problem you are having with your computer, and this software support download will solve it." You are underwriting those promises, and customers will hold you accountable to them.

Knowing what your customers expect is the first step to creating Knock Your Socks Off Service. By asking questions of your customers and your colleagues, and really listening, you'll be able to discover the details of the Service Promise your customers expect you to fulfill.

Managing Promises

The service promise can and should be managed. Once you know what your customers do and don't expect—the promise they want you to make—you are in a position to shape your customers' expectations to match what you actually can and will do for them. When you do that well, customers judge you and your organization to be reliable.

Let's say you are a salesperson in a store selling custom-built furniture. Jane Dowe comes in looking for a desk and credenza. She's never purchased custom-built furniture before, and she assumes—has an expectation—that you have most models in stock and that she'll be able to take her purchase home with her today. Your challenge is to change her expectations to match what your organization can do for her.

You show your organization's promise—commitment to quality products—by leading her to several sample desks

and credenzas on the show floor. Perhaps there is even a display showing the custom manufacturing process. You reinforce the organization's message with a personal promise: "Our custom desks allow us to combine the features that best meet your needs with the highest quality craftsmanship. If we can finalize the design today, I can have your desk delivered in two weeks."

Now Jane has a clear understanding of the service promise. She may decide that the wait is worth it because of the quality involved. If she really needs the desk today—in which case, you can't change her expectations *this* time—at least she will leave your store knowing the difference between custom made and off-the-shelf, and knowing that you are concerned with her satisfaction. And she may recommend you to a friend or colleague based on her revised understanding of your capabilities.

Fixing Promises When They Break

Sometimes promises made in good faith can't be kept. As much as we strive to be error-free, it's inevitable that problems will occur. Not everything that affects your customer's experience with you is within your control. What should you do when the Service Promise is broken? Job number one is to apologize, ideally contacting customers before they contact you. Don't waste time scapegoating—blaming yourself, your company, or your customer. Admit that something has gone wrong, and immediately find out what your customer needs now. Has the broken promise created another problem? Or has it, perhaps, created an opportunity for you to rescue your reputation for reliability?

> **TIP:** Never overpromise just to get the sale. In today's service-sensitive economy, service doesn't end with the sale, it just begins. Keeping the promises you make and only making promises you can keep is what reliability is all about.

For example, suppose Jane Dowe, the desk buyer, understands that her delivery will take two weeks, but you've just found out that deliveries are running about three days behind schedule. If you don't call with the bad news, you can bet she'll call you when the desk doesn't arrive on the day she was told to expect it—and she won't be happy about the delay. However, if you take the initiative and call her yourself, you might discover that the delay is acceptable. Or, if she has an important meeting and needs furniture in her office on that specific day, you can arrange for a loaner until the order arrives. Then, you (and your company) look like a hero.

Consistency and Predictability

A big part of reliability comes from the repetition of the customer experience. When the customer always has the same "wow" experience, there develops the perception of consistency of service. Regardless of where the customer enters the organization, the experience should be the same. If she is asking questions via Web chat, the quality of the service experience sets a standard of expectation. When the same customer has to call about a return or to see if the item is available from another location, that previous encounter sets the standard of expectation. If the new experience is at the same level, or higher, the customer perceives the organization as consistently delivering high-quality service. From this point, the customer might predict how her next interaction is likely to go. Here's the "predictability" component. If what the customer experiences is erratic in quality, you get low marks for consistency, predictability, and overall reliability.

> "You can't promise your customers sunny weather, but you can promise to hold an umbrella over them when it rains."

> —Sign in a telephone service center

4

Knock Your Socks Off Service Is:

(Re)-Assuring The Assurance Factor

"Consistent, high-quality service boils down to two equally important things: caring and competence."

—Chip R. Bell and Ron Zemke
Service Wisdom

In many companies, the desire to improve service quality has given birth to countless hours of "smile training," as though the key to satisfying every customer's needs and expectations involved nothing more than a cheery greeting and a happy-face sticker. Today's customer service professionals know that there's much more involved in creating customer satisfaction than smiles and happy faces.

If being nice were the complete answer, good service would be the norm, but that's clearly not the case. Make no mistake: Courtesy, good manners, and civility are important—treat your customers like dirt and they'll make your life miserable every time. But courtesy is not a substitute for competence and skill.

18

Consider the service technician who is friendly and accommodating on the phone, but who can't for the life of him figure out how to restore your lost Internet connection or eliminate the virus plaguing your Outlook software. Or the employee at the home improvement store who cheerfully walks you over to the product bin you were searching for, but then is at a loss about what kind of part you need to repair your leaky pipe. While both servers might get high marks for attitude, their lack of product knowledge makes for a less-than-satisfying service encounter.

When you provide Knock Your Socks Off Service, your actions assure customers that they are doing business with a well-trained, skillful service professional. Customers know they can trust you because of the competence and confidence you display in your work.

Today, customers expect to be reassured—to be made to feel comfortable—by the people they deal with. And that takes more than mastery of a few simple "people skills." It's the combination of both style and substance that wins accolades and brings customers back again and again.

Bad Service Drives Customers Away

Knock Your Socks Off Service professionals know that inept service has profound consequences. One study on retailing reports that customers identify "salespeople who know less about their products than I do" as a leading reason for switching from shopping at department stores to shopping via web sites or catalogs. Another study in the automobile industry finds that two out of three car buyers refuse to return to the same dealership for their next car. Their reasons have little to do with the car itself and more to do with the sleight-of-hand salesmanship encountered on the showroom floor and the boorish treatment they encountered when they brought the family chariot in for service. Thanks to the vast amount of comparative data available on the Internet, the number of customers who know more about your products than you do is higher than ever before. According to Chip Horner, vice president of Pfizer Consumer Group in Morris Plains, New Jersey, "Customers have done a lot more research, they go to the Web, and they save the toughest questions for the phone call or the e-mail to our call centers. Some of those questions are so obscure that we have to be prepared for the unexpected in much more detail."

This is why providing Knock Your Socks Off Service has such a positive impact on your company, on your customer, and on your career. Good service providers stand out, so make yourself memorable. Combine substance and style—what you do and how you do it—to reassure your customers that you really do know, and care about, what you are doing.

The Reassurance Factor

The reassurance factor is about managing your customers' feelings of trust. The customer's decision to trust you is built on your honesty, knowledge, and know-how. It is the substance that backs up your style, and it comes in four packages:

1. *Product Knowledge.* Customers expect you to know the features, advantages, and benefits of whatever it is your company makes, does, or delivers. The salesperson who has to read the manual in front of the customer just to figure out how to use the digital camera or netbook doesn't create an impression of

competence. It's helpful to know your products and how they compare to the products of your competition. So, some industry knowledge may help to set you apart in a positive way.

2. *Company Knowledge.* Customers expect you to know more than the limits of your particular job. They expect you to know how your organization works so you can guide them to someone who can meet their needs if those needs should fall outside your area of responsibility. Can you help your customer navigate the briar patch that is your business easily and successfully?

3. *Listening Skills.* Customers expect you to listen, understand, and respond to their specific needs as they explain them to you. They expect you to ask pertinent questions that will enable them to provide you with the information you need so that you may effectively meet their needs. They expect you to pay attention and get it right so they don't have to repeat it. And they expect you to tell the truth when a thing can't be done—or done in the time frame they want.

4. *Problem-Solving Skills.* Customers expect that you will be able to recognize their needs as they express them and quickly align them with the services your organization provides. And when things go wrong or don't work, they expect you to know how to fix things . . . and fix them fast.

Extra Points for Style

A competent annual physical performed by a rude, disheveled, or distracted physician isn't likely to be a satisfying experience for the patient, regardless of the technical excellence of the doctor. Once you've mastered the fundamentals of competence, it's your confident style that sets you apart. It starts with first impressions. In their classic book, *Contact: The First Four Minutes* (Ballantine Books, 1976), Leonard and Natalie Zunin contend that "the first four minutes of any contact is a kind of audition." In some customer service situations, you may have far less time than that: many transactions today are over in twenty to sixty seconds.

But first impressions are only the beginning. In service, everything communicates your style to customers. The way you dress, the way you move, or whether you move at all instead of staying barricaded behind a desk or cash register. The way you talk, your e-mail greeting, the way you do or don't make eye contact, listen, and respond. The way you act when you're not taking care of customers but are still within their view. And the way you take care of the person ahead of them in line.

Caring service, delivered quickly and confidently by knowledgeable, courteous people—what more could your customers want?

> "I always wanted to fully understand the situation before I made a commitment. It finally dawned on me that my customer needs the reassurance of my commitment before he'll give me time to understand the problem."
>
> —Customer Service Representative, Semiconductor Manufacturing Company

5

Knock Your Socks Off Service Is:

Tangibles

"From the customer's point of view, if they can see it, walk on it, hold it, hear it, step in it, smell it, carry it, step over it, touch it, use it, even taste it, if they can feel it or sense it, it's customer service."

—SuperAmerica Training Program

Service is difficult to describe in tangible, physical terms. It's fuzzy. Mushy. Slippery. You can't bottle a trip to the movies or an appendectomy any more than you can put a yardstick to advice from a stockbroker or ideas from an interior decorator. Twenty minutes with a physician or auto mechanic isn't necessarily better or worse than ten minutes or thirty minutes. It's the quality of what is accomplished, not the quantity of the time involved. One of the major complications in providing service comes from the fact that so much of it is intangible.

Yet in every service encounter there are tangibles before, during, and after the fact that affect the way customers judge the quality of the service you're providing. If you work in a hotel and a customer asks you for directions to an off-property restaurant and you point the way, that's intangible. Drawing a map is a way to make the service tangible. Having a preprinted map and specific directions at the ready is both tangible and Knock Your Socks Off Service performance! The third key to mastering the fundamentals of Knock Your Socks Off Service is understanding the role tangibles play in making your intangible service memorable and satisfying.

Think about going out for dinner:

- *Before* you enter a restaurant, you evaluate it based on some of its tangible attributes: the advertising you've seen or heard, the location as you drive up, and the cleanliness of the parking lot where you leave your car. Can you smell the aroma of good food or the remains of half-eaten meals rotting in the dumpster? Do the building and grounds look well kept? Is the sign lit and legible?
- *As you walk through the front door*, you make more judgments. Does the host or hostess look friendly? Does the establishment appear to be clean? (And if it's not, do you really want to eat the food?) Is there a place to hang or check your coat? Can you find the restrooms without a guide?
- *During* your meal, you evaluate other tangibles, from standard expectations about the menu and the tableware to unique items such as the special hat you see a server give a small child or the balloons passed out to a group celebrating a birthday. You judge the way your food is presented—how it looks on the plate and how closely it resembles the wonderful picture you saw on the menu—as well as how it tastes.
- *Afterward,* there are still more forms of tangible evidence for you to weigh. When the bill arrives, is it clean, accurate, and clearly understandable, or do you get the impression that it absorbed more of your meal than you did? If you use the restroom, is it clean? And if you paid your $19.01 bill with a twenty, did your server bring you 99 cents in change or a crisp, new single?

Demonstrating Value

Tangibles help convey the value of the service transaction's intangible aspects. They're an important way for you to educate your customers and help them evaluate the quality of service you've provided. Manage the tangible aspects of the service encounter and you give your customers something solid to tie their impressions to.

> **TIP:** If you're helping a customer estimate the cost of a purchase, be it a new home theater system, a pair of eyeglasses, or a roomful of carpet, write your calculations neatly on a page with your name, phone number, and e-mail address. Your customer will appreciate having it as a reference and will easily remember who provided such terrific service.

Here are four ways you can manage tangibles in your own environment to make a positive impression on customers:

1. Take pride in your own appearance and the look and feel of the materials you give to your customer. Hand them

over personally instead of tossing them on a countertop or leaving it to the customer to figure out what to gather up and how to organize or carry them. If you're sending order confirmations, price quotes, or other information to customers via e-mail or text, make sure documents or messages are easy to read, presented in a professional manner, grammatically correct, and error-free. Treat your materials with respect and customers will respect—and remember positively—what you have done for them.

2. When customers give you their name, phone number, e-mail address, web site, or other information, write it down or add it to your contacts list or other device immediately. This demonstrates that you think the information is important. Make a point of getting it right—read it back to make sure there's no mistake. And remember that many customers today are nervous about who has their personal information. Be sure they see you safeguarding it.

3. Make sure the parts of your workplace customers see— and especially those they touch—are clean, safe, and as comfortable as you can make them.

4. Provide customers with e-mail confirmation. Even though many customers are comfortable and familiar with Internet shopping, most still appreciate being able to print out a hard copy receipt and confirmation of their product or service orders. Others just want to know that you received an e-mail they sent, and if you can't respond immediately to their question, when you anticipate being able to send an answer. Fingertip access to this information eases customers' minds should follow-up be required.

When your customers describe your service to their friends and colleagues—people who could become your next customers—they will focus on their observations of tangible things. To keep customers coming back again and again, you want those tangibles to reflect well on you and the service you provide.

"First impressions are the most lasting."

—Proverb

6

Knock Your Socks Off Service Is:

Empathetic

Customers come in a wide variety of shapes and sizes, and they bring an equally wide variety of wants, needs, expectations, attitudes, and emotions with them to the service transaction. Consequently, customers want to be treated as individuals. No one likes to be treated like a number by a service worker responding like a machine. Recognizing your customers' emotional states helps you figure out the best way to effectively and professionally serve them.

Consider how you might treat these two customers if you were the banquet manager for a fancy hotel:

- Tom Timid walks into the catering office looking nervous and tense. He is planning a special retirement party for his boss of ten years and he's obviously never organized a function like this before.
- Demanding Doris is an old hand at hosting special events. The annual sales department gala will be the fourth major event she has organized this year. When she

walks into the banquet office, Doris knows exactly what she wants. Her you-all-just-stand-back-and-take-orders attitude is clearly visible.

How do you treat Tom and Doris as individuals? For Tom, it is important to make him comfortable and take the time to make him "feel smart" about the event planning process and supported by you:

> "Tom, you can depend on me to be there every step of the way. To begin with, why don't you tell me a little bit more about your event, and then I'll walk you through our step-by-step planning process."

The same technique would probably frustrate or even anger Doris. She may see your friendly, in-depth explanation as a waste of her valuable time. She expects you to credit her with the savvy she has shown on previous occasions:

> "Hello, Doris. It's good to work with you again. I see you brought an outline of everything you need. You always make my job so much easier! Let me take a quick look and see if I have any questions."

Seeing and treating each customer as an individual helps you meet the needs of each on their own unique level.

Good? They knocked my socks off and wrinkled my panty hose.

Empathy vs. Sympathy

Whatever the emotional state of your customers—cautious or confident—it's important to each of them that you understand what they're trying to tell you and how they feel about the services they want you to provide. But when emotions run high—especially when things are going wrong—it's easy to get caught up in a customer's emotional world.

When responding to customers' emotions, it's helpful to make a distinction between *empathy* and *sympathy*. Both have to do with how you respond to other people's emotions. Many people use the terms interchangeably, but the difference is real and important.

- *Sympathy* involves identifying with, and even taking on, another person's emotions. A sympathetic response is, "I'm really angry about those centerpieces, too."
- *Empathy* means acknowledging and affirming another's emotional state. An empathetic response is, "I can see that you are really angry about how those centerpieces look."

TIP: When a service provider wallows in a customer's misfortune, there are two victims instead of one. As a service professional, you need to see the clear difference between what happened and who it happened to—and work on the former to bring things back to normal.

What's the Difference?

Responding to customers with sympathy—getting as upset as they are—puts you on an emotional roller coaster and can leave you worn out and frazzled at the end of the day. The trick is to be emotionally aware and sensitive without becoming too emotionally involved. When you respond with empathy, you stay calm and in control of yourself. Only then are you at your absolute best: ready, willing, and able to help your customer meet his needs or solve his problem.

Showing empathy for customers actually allows you to be professional and caring at the same time. It also makes customers feel like important individuals. Empathy cannot be handed out by a machine; it's something one person does for another. There is no substitute for the human touch you provide when you deliver Knock Your Socks Off Service. That's what makes high-quality service such hard work. It's also what makes it so rewarding.

Using empathy statements is a skill that comes naturally to some and can be learned by all. And, like all skills, practice makes us proficient. Try new skills in a safe environment first—at home or with your colleagues—before applying them to customers.

The steps that follow will help you craft your own unique empathy statements for service encounters. The key is to be genuine and sincere; your level of concern will shine through to customers.

Building Empathy Statements

- Lead-in
  - I hear that. . .
  - I see that. . .
  - It's clear to me that. . .
- Acknowledgment of the other person
  - You. . .
  - I hear that you. . .
- Description of the feeling
  - Are: angry; frustrated; anxious; disappointed; nervous; confused; surprised
- Description of the situation
  - Because. . .(content of the message)

> **TIP 2:** Practice creating empathy statements that are unique to your customers by using the Building Empathy Statements guide

Here are some examples of empathy statements in action:

"It is clear by your voice that you are frustrated by the number of call transfers that have taken place."

"I hear the frustration that you think no one can solve your problem."

"I see that you are surprised by the change in our return policy since you last shopped with us."

TIP: Demonstrate empathy by listening for and using the customer's name, referring to something in his history with your company, and thanking him for his continued patronage. Make it special and unique for each customer.

Customers appreciate personal attention demonstrated by caring, knowledgeable professionals. Connecting on an emotional level provides the kind of service that customers are likely to long remember and cherish.

"Customers don't care how much you know, until they know how much you care."

—Digital Equipment Corp.
Customer Service Department

7

Knock Your Socks Off Service Is:

Responsive

"A rose on time is far more valuable than a $1,000 gift that's too late."

—Jim Rohn
Author and motivational speaker

Timeliness has always been important. And today, responsive action—doing things in a timely fashion—is even more crucial. Just look around at the number of businesses that have been created to get things done quickly:

- FedEx won international success by delivering letters and small parcels "Absolutely, Positively, Anytime."
- LensCrafters optical stores promise "Custom-Crafted Eyeglasses in About an Hour."
- Google built its success on providing instant access to a vast universe of information at the click of a mouse.
- Zappos.com will have shoes arriving on your doorstep the very next day because they value your time and want you to come back to their site again and again.

The big-name national service leaders don't have a corner on the timeliness market. All over town, you can find same-day dry cleaning, carpet installed the next day, and twenty-four-hour automated banking services. At the same time, a growing number of traditional manufacturing companies are practicing Just-In-Time (JIT) inventory management, ordering things to arrive just in time. Sometimes "just in the nick of time."

Companies that cater to time-conscious customers are everywhere you look. With software programs that now continuously search the Internet for mentions of a company, service providers can respond to a post or Tweet practically before the customer's fingers leave his or her keyboard. And their success affects your customers' expectations of your willingness and ability to do the same. Small wonder that your customers may be demanding tighter deadlines and faster service than ever before. When they see others promising—and delivering—fast, fast, fast, they expect the same from you.

Setting—and Meeting—Deadlines

Sometimes it seems that everybody wants everything done at the same time. But it's a mistake to automatically think your customers won't accept anything less than "right this instant." On the other hand, giving yourself too much extra "wiggle room" or time to do the work can make you appear slow and leave you and your company looking unresponsive.

Start by finding out what the customer really needs by when. There's a big difference between, "I have to have this dry-cleaned to wear in two days" and, "I want to have these winter coats cleaned before I put them away for the season." Use that information to pick a time that works well for you and try it out on the customer. Nine times out of ten, you'll hear "yes." And if your suggestion doesn't work, your customer will let you know and you can work together to find an alternative. Customers appreciate and remember such responsiveness to their needs.

> **TIP:** The next time you're in doubt, ask your customers, "When would you like this?" You may be pleasantly surprised when they pick a reasonable

time, or even ask you: "Well, when could you have
it done?" An added benefit is that it gives them a
sense of control and involvement. We are all more
comfortable when we feel we have some control
over our lives and the things that go on around us.

Deadlines are important. But deadlines are created by people. When you say to a customer, "I'll have it ready for you this
afternoon," or, "I'll put it in the mail today," you are creating
an expectation for your customer and setting a deadline for
yourself. Be realistic, because once created, deadlines become
yardsticks by which your customer will measure your success
or failure. Knock Your Socks Off Service results from creating
acceptable, realistic expectations of responsiveness in your
customers' minds and then meeting those expectations.

When Customers Must Wait

The best time for anything is the time that is best for the customer. But dissatisfaction isn't always measured in minutes.
Rather, dissatisfaction is often the result of uncertainty.
Research shows that the most frustrating aspect of waiting is
not knowing how long the wait will be. Better to be proactive
than reactive.

A friend of ours recently took her car to be serviced early
on a Monday morning. After not hearing any updates all day,
she finally called the repair shop late Monday afternoon and
was upset to learn mechanics hadn't even looked at it yet.
She'd taken the day off work and could've been running
errands all day instead of being without a vehicle. A little information up front would have saved her time—and the repair
shop a customer!

Be aware of what your customers think is an acceptable
wait. According to a study by *Restaurants & Institutions* magazine, for example, "fast" for fast-food customers means five
minutes or less, while diners in a family restaurant are willing
to wait as long as thirty minutes for their specially prepared
food to arrive. Similarly, in the retail business expectations

may vary with the time of day or season of the year. Customers are less able, let alone less willing, to wait around for help during their lunch hour at work than on a lazy Sunday afternoon.

> **TIP:** Pay special attention to waiting time when your customers are out of your sight, whether on the phone, in another part of town, or in another state, rather than standing right in front of you. Out of sight is much more worrisome to customers.

Think about your own experiences as a customer. When you are in line behind someone who insists on paying off the national debt in pennies or are waiting for the manufacturer to plant and grow the oak trees to make your new furniture, it is usually the uncertainty—Will I be served sometime this century?—more than the wait itself that gets your blood pumping. Ditto for sitting on an airplane as your scheduled departure time goes whooshing by. The wait is more tolerable if the pilot announces the reason for the delay, rather than leaving you wondering if or when the wheels will ever again leave the tarmac.

As a service professional, you may not be able to count pennies any faster, make trees grow overnight, or get an airplane off the ground, but you can make waiting less traumatic. Acknowledge waiting customers and keep them informed about what is happening. Be as specific as you can: "I'm with another customer right now, but should be free in about fifteen minutes. If you would like to look around some more, I'll come find you the minute I'm through."

In face-to-face settings, acknowledgment doesn't have to be verbal. In the words of one restaurateur, "Make eye contact with the customers. Make your actions say, 'I know you are there. I'll be with you very soon.'"

"Our customer support is so responsive that. . .Oops, there's a call, gotta go!"

—Advertisement for an Internet Service Provider

8

The Customer Is Always . . .

The Customer

Our Policy
Rule 1: The customer is always right!
Rule 2: If the customer is ever wrong, reread Rule 1.

—Stew Leonard's Dairy Store
Norwalk, Connecticut

These words, chiseled into a 6,000-pound rock resting just outside the front door of Stew Leonard's, the world's largest (and most profitable) dairy store, are probably familiar.

They are also wrong.

So why do the people who run Stew Leonard's Dairy so loudly proclaim "Rule 1" and "Rule 2" at the entrance to the store? Because each and every employee knows, lives, and breathes the real truth behind the slogan written on the rock: Customers are not always right, but they are *always* our customers.

Right and Wrong

The customer is not always right. You know it. We know it. In fact, studies conducted by Arlington, Virginia–based TARP, a premier service research firm, even prove it scientifically. TARP finds that customers cause about a third of the service and product problems they complain about. Blindly believing or acting as if you believe the customer is always right can be detrimental to you and to your customer.

Caution: Customers-are-always-right thinking can put a stop to problem solving and customer education. You can't correct a problem or a customer's misconception if you can't admit that it exists. Many times when customers cause problems—or believe untrue things—it's because we haven't taught them any differently. We are so familiar with the products we sell and the services we supply that we forget how much there is to know, how much we have to help our customers learn.

Perhaps more dangerous is that customers-are-always-right thinking puts service providers in a one-down position. It says, "You're not paid to think or ask questions. Just smile and do whatever the customer tells you to do." No wonder that in such settings, service begins to feel like servitude: "Hello, my name is Pat and I'll be your personal slave this evening," is a bad mindset.

Finally, blindly holding to the idea that customers are always right means that when something goes wrong—as it will, sooner or later—*you* as the server must be wrong. You know that's not true. If you're behind the counter in a Mc-Donald's and a customer walks up and orders McLobster and a bottle of McChampagne, it's very clear who's right and who's wrong. It's also irrelevant. Your job is to manage the encounter so the customer continues to be a customer. As in, "We're McOut of those two items but we have some other great things to eat here on our menu board."

Why We're There

The customer is our only reason for being there. Knowing that the customer is always the customer (not the problem, the enemy, or the bane of your existence) helps focus your effort where it belongs—on keeping the customer. The goal of every service transaction is, and must be, to satisfy and delight customers in ways that will keep them coming back for more.

As a service professional, you hold the power to make that happen. To do it, you need to be and act smart. You need to know more than your customer does about the products and services you sell and supply. You need to be sensitive to the fact that customers, like service professionals, are only human, with human faults and feelings. When customers are wrong, your role is to use your skills to help make them right, in a manner that neither embarrasses nor blames.

Three Ways to Make Customers Right

1. *Assume innocence.* "Guilty until proven innocent" doesn't play well with customers. Just because what they are saying sounds wrong to you, don't assume that it is. It may be that they are simply explaining what they need or want poorly, or that the directions they should have received were missing or misleading. Choose your words carefully:

> "I see what happened. This disc is a CD-R, not a CD-RW. Information can only be saved to it once, not over and over. Here's what I can do. . ."

2. *Look for teaching opportunities.* What information could your customers have used before the misunderstanding occurred? Make sure they get it now.

> "I'm glad you brought this to my attention. The information you needed was here in your packet, but I can see how it would be easy to miss, buried under so many other papers. Let's review your packet to see if I can head off any other surprises."

Or

> "I'm sorry you aren't happy with your Pez® dispenser, but the head is supposed to go back like

that—that's how the candy is dispensed. I would be happy to refund your money, if that's what you'd like."

TIP: You can't educate the irate. When they are stressed and angry, customers do not take kindly to reeducation—"You know, you could have avoided all of this if you'd just remembered to ...." Choosing to educate at the wrong moment is a sure way to add to the customer's unhappiness. Look for ways to avoid embarrassing the customer when he or she has made a mistake or misunderstood something.

3. *Believe your customer.* Sometimes, the customer you initially think is 100 percent wrong will turn out to be right— or at least partly right—after all. They might, for instance, just be having difficulty providing a clear explanation of the problem. If you've ridden roughshod over their request or complaint, you're going to find yourself wolfing down a heaping helping of humble pie. The point of Knock Your Socks Off Service is to keep customer relationships intact. When in doubt, give your customer the benefit of the doubt.

"Let's check the advertising flyer to verify that the price you saw is for this model. Sure enough, there it is. Thanks for pointing that out to me. I'll make sure we get the shelf tags corrected so everyone knows which model is on sale."

Unfair Advantage

What about customers who try to use your service standards against you and get something for nothing or a better deal than they are entitled to? First, it's important to recognize that truly dishonest customers are pretty rare. But they do exist. Much more common are customers who honestly disagree with you about what is true and what is fair.

How do you tell the difference between legitimate and deceitful customer actions? We recommend opting for some version of the "three strikes and you're out" policy. The first time a customer and clerk disagree on whether a video was returned on time, take ownership, and let the fee slide. Do it again the second time—give your customer the benefit of the doubt. But three strikes, and the customer's credibility is gone and the late charge stands.

> **NOTE:** Making a wrong customer right, without giving away the store, can be an incredible challenge. In fact, we wrote an entire book about it— *Knock Your Socks Off Service Recovery* (AMACOM, 1997), It's a great desk reference for figuring out tactful responses to customers.

"Don't fix the blame. Fix the problem."
—Japanese saying

II

The How To's of Knock Your Socks Off Service

Outstanding customer service is a tapestry of individual actions that are important in the customer's eyes. Most are relatively easy and simple to master. Woven together, they make the service you provide truly memorable.

How well you listen, understand, and respond to each customer, how you handle face-to-face contact, how you use the telephone, how you enter a Tweet or respond on instant chat, the words you put on paper or in e-mail messages, and the way you anticipate customer needs all contribute to your customer's evaluations of your efforts.

Properly combined and skillfully executed, these elements add up to outstanding service, the kind that says, "I'm gonna knock your socks off!"

9

Honesty Is the Only Policy

"A man always has two reasons for doing anything—a
good reason, and the real reason."

—J. P. Morgan, financier

When it comes to customer service, honesty isn't the best policy, it is the <u>only</u> policy. Lying to or misleading customers invariably leads to far worse problems than looking them straight in the eye and telling them something unpleasant they need to hear right now.

There are two very good reasons for facing your customer with the bad news.

First, tall tales inevitably catch up with you, and often in the most unexpected ways. Tom Connellan, president of the Orlando-based Connellan Group, tells the story of a shipping clerk (let's call him Ralph) in a company in Michigan who had discovered a cute and, to his way of thinking, foolproof way of keeping customers off his back. Every morning he would bring three newspapers to work: the *New York Daily News,* the *Chicago Tribune,* and the *Los Angeles Times.* He would scan each carefully and circle any news item having to do with a transportation disaster—train wrecks and derailments, heavy snowfall in the Rocky Mountains, trucking strikes in the Southeast. You get the picture.

Then, for the rest of the day, any time a customer called up complaining that a promised shipment had not yet arrived, Ralph would put the caller on hold, thumb through the

newspapers until he found a likely item, go back to the caller
and ask: "Did you hear about the train that derailed outside
Fort Worth last night? No? Well, it happened, and I know for
a fact that your shipment was on that train. I'd like to help
you out, but there's not a thing I can do about delays that are
out of my control. I'm sure you understand."

Ralph's little trick worked well for all of a year—until a customer, suspicious of the fact that three of his last five promised
shipments were subject to "disasters," began checking around.
To make a long story short, he figured out what Ralph was up
to, put Ralph's company on his "Unreliable Vendor" list, and
wrote a stinging letter to Ralph's company president. Do you
need to ask what kind of disaster happened to Ralph?

The second reason for playing straight with your customers is that—surprise!—customers respect honesty. No, it
isn't fun to tell a customer that there is a problem, or that the
delivery date the customer has in mind is unrealistic. But
when you have to be candid, and you make it clear how you'll
follow up to make things right, your customers come away ap-
preciating you as a straight shooter they can depend on to tell
the truth—regardless.

Miss Manners, a.k.a. Judith Martin, dubbed The High
Priestess of Protocol by *Frequent Flyer* magazine, provides a
case in point. She described two recent airline flights, both de-
layed due to bad weather. As she described them to the readers of *Frequent Flyer*:

> On the first, the crew did little to inform the passen-
> gers of the flight's status, glumly responding to
> requests for pillows, blankets, drinks, etc.

> The second crew apologized for the delay, offered
> advice on passengers' scheduling problems, kept ev-
> eryone informed, and generally tried to make things
> as pleasant as possible.

Which planeload of passengers believed that the flight
crew was really doing everything possible to get them to their
destination? And which airline will Miss Manners choose the
next time she flies?

Do It for Yourself, Too

There is actually a third reason for always being honest with customers: the way you feel about yourself. A friend of ours used to work for a now defunct television shopping network company. She was the chief upset customer handler. When customers called to report that the merchandise they bought was defective, her job was to smother those callers with platitudes like "I'm sorry" and "We apologize."

The trouble was, most of the merchandise the company was selling was factory seconds—items known by everyone in the company to be defective in some small way. Our friend was, in essence, a shill charged with the responsibility of mollifying the few customers who were brave enough to complain about their purchases. The company, she was told straight out, was counting on the fact that only about 4 percent of upset customers complain when they receive shoddy service or merchandise.

Did she give the complainers their money back? Absolutely. The company was willing to buy off the few who braved its complaint and return systems. Did she make the complainers feel better? Definitely. At least someone was there to listen to them.

TIP: How you feel about yourself in your job is as important to your self-esteem as the way you feel

about yourself as a parent, a spouse, or a friend.
No job is important enough to lie for, no paycheck
big enough to compensate for feeling bad about
your treatment of another human being. Perhaps
the best reason to be honest with your customers
is that it allows you to be honest with yourself.

But she quit her job after six months. Why? "Because,"
she says, "I couldn't take being part of an operation that was
knowingly exploiting its customers."

"Whoever is careless with the truth in small matters
cannot be trusted with important matters."
—Albert Einstein

10

All Rules Were Meant to Be Broken

(Including This One)

"Rules exist to serve, not enslave."

—Software programmer's axiom

Rules are everywhere. We encounter formal rules in the form of laws and policies—"No right turn on red," or "Returns must be accompanied by receipt." Other rules are informal, taught by custom or experience—"When you bump into another person, say 'Excuse me,'" or "Allow extra time when driving during rush hour."

Rules should share a single purpose: to make life run in a more efficient, organized, and orderly fashion. We sometimes call this purpose the spirit of the law. But rules don't always fulfill their spirit. In fact, sometimes they work against what we're trying to accomplish. That's why it's important for Knock Your Socks Off Service professionals to understand the rules that direct their efforts.

Rules vs. Assumptions

We are so used to rules in our lives that sometimes, when we don't know the answer or aren't comfortable making a decision of our own, we're tempted to make up a rule to fill the gap. Or, in the stress of the moment, we may borrow a rule from another setting that seems to fit our current situation.

For example, imagine you're a new cashier. A customer comes in and asks to write a check for $20 more than the amount of purchase. You don't know what your store policy is, and there's no one nearby to ask. What do you do?

- You might assume that cashing checks for over the amount is against the rules and say no.
- Or you may borrow a rule from your last job and allow the customer to write the check for $5 or $10 more.

Either option is tempting because it puts you in control of the situation and keeps you from having to say, "Gee, I don't know if you can do that." But not knowing all the rules is natural! In fact, not knowing and finding out—for yourself and for the customer—is one of the best ways to learn on the job. Instead of assuming there must be a rule that will make you say no, find out how to say yes.

A friend of ours remembers a business trip to Kansas City. She was working particularly long days. Back in her hotel room one evening, hungry from having skipped lunch, she reviewed the room service menu. Nothing appealed. She called down to room service and asked if she could have a plain broiled chicken breast with a small salad. "I don't see that on the menu," the room service waiter responded. "It's not," she replied, "but it's what I'd really like to have. Can you make it?" Silence. Then again, "Well, it's not on the menu." To make a long story short, she didn't end up with a room service meal that night, though the room service personnel at many hotels since then have easily and cheerfully accommodated similar requests. Guess which hotel in Kansas City she tells people to avoid?

Red Rules vs. Blue Rules

Rules are important when they protect the public safety or reflect experience that says dire consequences will occur if the wrong things happen. But other rules are simply habits and customs with hardened arteries—systems that grow inflexible with age and take on a rigidity never intended.

In healthcare, some organizations we know of explain to employees that there are two kinds of rules—Red rules and Blue rules: *Red rules* are rules that cannot be broken. They are there to protect the life or well-being of the patient; for example, no smoking on the premises. *Blue rules* are designed to make the hospital experience run more smoothly for patient and staff alike. For example: Incoming patients are processed through the Admitting Department.

Healthcare workers have to know when a Blue rule, such as "Fill out the admission forms first," should or must be broken. For example, in the emergency room when a pregnant woman arrives in labor, the paperwork can wait.

Do you know the Red rules and the Blue rules in your company? Red rules may be set by the government in the form of laws or regulations, or by your company's management. Blue rules may evolve from department policy or past experience. You need to understand where the rules come from and why they exist and be able to explain them to your customers so they in turn know why you're doing what you're doing.

TIP: As you discuss Red rules and Blue rules in your own organization there are bound to be disagreements about which is which. That's okay. A key outcome of your Red and Blue discussion is learning why a rule is a rule in the first place. For example, some employees at a large insurance company were upset to learn that using personal software programs such as screensavers and games on company computers was a violation of a Red rule—actually a firing offense. After a very public e-mail dialog with the Information Services group about why the rule existed, most employees came to agree that there was indeed a danger of introducing a computer virus into the system. Now the color of that particular rule makes sense to everyone in the company.

Breaking vs. Bending the Rules

Know your own limits. If you believe an exception should be made but aren't sure you can or should do it, ask a more experienced peer, your supervisor, or your manager.

Given the speed of communication today via Twitter, online chat programs, and even social networks, knowing the rules becomes even more important. When you are given the authority to respond to customers through these mediums, you are making split-second decisions for both the customer and the company. The more you know, the more comfortable you will be in these situations.

Without formal and informal rules, service would become chaotic—and customers would never know what to expect. Just because you think that breaking or bending a rule won't cause the ceiling to fall doesn't mean you should take it lightly. Know the nature of the rule in question, the reason for the rule, and the consequences of not following it—then help your customer make the system work.

"The exception proves the rule."
—Seventeenth century proverb

11

Creating Trust in an Insecure, Suspicious World

"Give trust, and you'll get it double in return."

—Kees Kamies

Trust is the platinum standard of customer service. It is the glue that keeps customers coming back. The customer's faith in your word and belief in your promises are what saves you in those difficult times when everything seems to be going wrong. If you have made promises in the past and things have turned out well, the customer will trust you when things go from good to bad to worse.

Customer trust grows slowly, develops over time, and is a succession of positive experiences. Trust can be dashed by a single incident of unfaithfulness and can be cemented by a singular memorable act.

Fairness is one of the customer's most critical trust-creating hot buttons. Treat me unfairly—from my point of view—and lose me forever as a client. Give my concerns a fair and thorough hearing and win my continued loyalty. What is fairness from the customer's point of view? That can and often does vary from customer to customer. But in general customers feel treated fairly when:

- They feel listened to and respected, even if they don't always get the exact outcome they are seeking.

53

- The process of getting what they want—of achieving a satisfying outcome—was painless.
- You kept the performance promises you made—if you said you'd call by the end of the day, you did.
- You treated them ethically; no bait and switch, no sneaky behavior.
- You acknowledged their unique wishes, if there were any.
- Their best interests were placed ahead of the company's convenience.

Example

It's 3 P.M. Friday afternoon. Mrs. Impulsive calls your travel agency. She just has to be in San Francisco by noon tomorrow. You warn her it could be expensive, but you'll do your best. An hour later you have a nonrefundable, coach class, excursion fare ticket on a 6 A.M. flight in hand. You call her with the news.

How Do You Build Trust?

Trust builds slowly, over time and by positive experiences. But there are some things you can do to speed trust along.

- *Practice frequent communications.* "Mrs. I, this is pretty short notice, I don't know if I can succeed, but I'll give it my best."
- *Stick with the truth.* "Given the few flights available on Saturdays, I might not be able to find one. But I'll do everything I can. The chances I'll succeed are pretty good."
- *Develop openness.* "Good news! I had to ask for a little favor and I had to go ahead and book you immediately, but if you can make a 6 A.M. flight, it is going to work out."

- *Show warmth.* "I hope you have a wonderful time. I know your daughter is going to be so glad and so surprised you could make it."

There can be a fine line between fibbing to a customer and being reassuring. Telling the customer that "everything will be fine" when it might turn out otherwise is an unacceptable way of dealing with a situation. Being straightforward without overdramatizing risks or overemphasizing things that can go wrong is always a better course.

- *Show confidence.* If you seem hesitant to do what the customer wants done or unsure of yourself, you erode trust, even if you succeed. A simple, "I don't know if we can make that change this close to your flight, but let me take a look—can I call you right back or would you rather I just put you on hold?" goes a long way to demonstrate your confidence.
- *Above all, keep your promises.* Nothing shatters customer trust like failing to do what you say you'll do. The repairman who doesn't show up at the appointed hour or the bank employee who fails to call back by the promised time about the error on your monthly statement often won't get second chances to win the customer's trust. If you find yourself unable to keep promises, make sure you contact customers to let them know.

Trust and Recovery

The core of the psychological side of *service recovery*—fixing customer problems—is restoring trust; the customer's belief that you can and will keep the explicit and implicit promises you make. Dr. Kathleen Seiders, an associate professor of marketing at Boston College, says that trust is particularly at risk when customers feel *vulnerable*; that is, they perceive that all the power to set things right is in your hands and little or nothing is under their control. That sense of vulnerability—and the customer's reaction to a service breakdown—is the loudest when the customer feels he/she lacks the following:

> *Information.* They don't know what is going on, or how long it will take to set things right.
> *Expertise.* The customer couldn't fix the car or the computer or fouled-up the reservation on a bet. All the "smarts" are on your side of the table.
> *Freedom.* There is no option for fixing the problem aside from dealing with you. The customer perceives you as the only hope.
> *Recourse.* The customer perceives that when it comes to this computer or car or malady it's you or nobody. They may be free, contractually, to ask anyone else they can find to do the problem "fix," but there is no one else, or at least they see it that way.

Restoring trust is accomplished by involving the customer in solving the problem: "Tell me again exactly what was happening when the mower stopped," or "Can you give me a rundown on the history of this problem," reassuring the client that the problem is fixable and will be fixed.

When the customer feels vulnerable, trust is imperative.

—Leonard L. Berry
Service Expert

12

Taking Ownership of Your Service Encounters

"Use your good judgment in all situations.
There will be no additional rules."

—Nordstrom, Inc.
employee handbook

Consider for a moment how frustrating it is when you dial a company's toll-free number only to be greeted with an automated phone menu. Although the recorded voice might be friendly and constantly remind you that "you're a valued customer," you wait patiently without hearing the option you believe best meets your needs. Because you're limited to only the options offered, in frustration you select one that you think is close enough. When a voice answers, you explain the reason for your call. How do you feel with the response on the line is, "Gee, that's not this department. Let me transfer you. . . click"?

In a 2008 survey conducted by Convergys, the U.S. Customer Scorecard, 64 percent of respondents said that addressing customer needs on first contact is a key service differentiator. Solve the customer's problem or answer a question in one friendly and efficient phone call, Twitter interaction, or e-mail—with no transfers, long waits on hold, or need for callbacks—and satisfaction rises substantially.

An additional testament to responsiveness (we covered that in Chapter 7) is your willingness to take ownership of the customer. Even though the help the customer needs may not be within the context of your duties, if you are the point of contact to the customer, it's up to you to work with that customer. You can get the information and call the customer back or provide the response directly. Many companies tout their "one contact" service standard to tell customers, "We're here to help on your first contact." Avoid customer transfers whenever possible.

Receiving Gifts

A shift in perspective may help service providers view this ownership idea differently. When a customer takes time to contact your organization, that comment, suggestion, question, or complaint should be seen as a gift. Yes, a gift! A customer who could have simply walked away because of confusion, a problem, or a lack of information is taking time to tell you about the situation—and most importantly, giving you an opportunity to work with them. That's a real gift.

Doing the Right Things vs. Doing Things Right

Doing the right thing and doing things right are separate but equal issues in providing Knock Your Socks Off Service.

Doing things right deals with the process of getting work done—doing your job correctly, using technical skills and people skills, learning about your company's products and services, and being able to answer questions about how things work and why.

Doing the right thing is about deciding what the best thing to do is in a given situation. It involves making judgments about how to use your company's products and services on your customers' behalf—sometimes in ways they may not have asked for or even thought of. It is about deciding whether or not to comply with a customer request.

The Nordstrom employee handbook is almost legendary. Its elegantly simple, solitary rule is: "Use your good judgment in all situations." The lack of additional rules doesn't mean there's no direction. Nordstrom employees—those fabled Knock Your Socks Off Service professionals—are encouraged to use their managers for support when they're not sure what to do. In Nordstrom's words:

> "Please feel free to ask your department manager, store manager or division general manager any question at any time."

Of course, such a policy only works if managers treat questions as teaching opportunities rather than as annoyances—and at Nordstrom's you'll find leaders who are devoted to coaching employees. In orientation and training programs, Nordstrom people learn what doing the right thing means for the customers they will serve. Sometimes it means accepting a return with no questions asked or walking a customer to another department—even to a competitor's store—to find just the right clothing accessory. The result? From coast to coast, people tell stories about service, Nordstrom style. Even those who've never seen the inside of a Nordstrom store have heard the stories thanks to books like *The Nordstrom Way to Customer Service Excellence* by Robert Spector (Wiley, 2005) and *Fabled Service* by Betsy Sanders (Jossey-Bass, 1997) written about Nordstrom's. And just about the time they start to shake their heads and say things like, "Sure, but how long can they stay in business doing things like that?" someone adds the real clincher: Nordstrom regularly posts some of the highest sales per square foot in the retail industry. Not only does nobody do it better, nobody makes more money doing it right, either!

Is the Right Thing Ever Wrong?

Many front-line service workers and plenty of managers feel an instinctive fear of simple policies such as, "do the right thing." The fear is natural; for generations, we've been warned about the dire consequences of "giving the store away." But that fear is easily overcome when common sense and the competence that comes with experience are brought to bear on the subject.

> **TIP:** Take time—perhaps an hour every two weeks—to get together with your co-workers to learn from each other's experiences. Share stories of successes and failures with tough customer problems. The chances are very good that if you are having a problem with something, so are others.

Are you going to give the store away? Of course not, no more than Nordstrom's people do. It's pointless for your company to hire good people like you, train them well, and back them with customer-friendly systems and supportive management only to refuse them the opportunity (or see them decline the opportunity) to make good judgments on their customers' behalf. The system's not out of control; it is being controlled by *your* innate good sense. That's why your company has already entrusted you with its most priceless asset—customers, the very future of the business.

Your own good judgment applies in every industry. If you know your job, but aren't sure exactly what you should or shouldn't do in a particular situation, try asking yourself the following three questions and using your answers as a guide:

1. *Does the action violate a Red rule, or is it about bending a Blue rule?* (see Chapter 10 for a quick review of Red and Blue rules.) If a red rule is involved, you can generally stop right here. When housekeepers at St. Luke's Hospital in Milwaukee are asked by patients for water, they know to check first with the charge nurse. If the patient is on restricted fluids, the simple act of providing a glass of water violates a Red rule.

2. *If it involves a Blue rule, will bending or breaking the rule allow you to serve customers better?* The fact that you *can* bend a rule is not in and of itself a compelling argument that you *should* bend or abandon a Blue rule. Interior window

cleaning for the historic Foshay Tower in Minneapolis, Minnesota, has always been done during the work week, during normal business hours—a de facto Blue rule. While the building manager will happily schedule weekend service for tenants who need it, she first explains, "Our windows date from 1929. We prefer to clean during the week so that if we discover that a repair is needed, it can be done immediately. I don't want any tenant to suffer with a taped up or boarded up temporary fix."

3. *Who should make the final decision?* Find that person, and take action. In many cases, it will be you. Sometimes, especially when bending a Blue rule involves a risk or an added expense, you will need to involve a manager or supervisor. With your answers to questions 1 and 2, you will be able to offer your manager thoughtful perspective and an action plan.

> "If they (employees) make a wrong decision, that's something that can be corrected later. At least they acted in good faith. This is part of our commitment (to our customers)."
>
> —Isadore Sharp
> Chairman, Four Seasons Hotels

13

Become a Listening Post

"Whether your customer comes to you via the Internet, the front door, or the telephone, there is gold to mine in the knowledge gained from these interactions. Pay attention!"

—Ann Thomas and Jill Applegate
Authors, *Pay Attention! How to Listen, Respond and Profit from Customer Feedback*

Social media has truly revolutionized the opportunities to listen to customers beyond what anyone would have dreamed even ten years ago. These days, it is so easy for customers to comment on your company; it's also so easy for your company to listen. With today's myriad options for communication, there are many ways to listen. And, listening to customers is something Knock Your Socks Off Service providers must do. Knock Your Socks Off Service organizations also realize that there are nuggets of gold to be mined in this new voice of the customer. These companies also view their front-line service providers—whether they meet customers face to face or "meet" them by monitoring social media and the Internet (or do both, in smaller companies)—as the true gems in the customer service gold mine. That's you! Well before anyone else in the organization, you know about emerging problems with service quality, and the recurring issues or breakdowns that are driving customers into the embrace of the competition. In that sense, you are an essential "listening post" for the organization.

The Value of Listening

Most of us listen to only about 25 percent of what we hear. What happens to the other 75 percent? We tune it out. In one ear and out the other. Listening is so important, it's amazing how seldom we practice it. But since good service involves listening, understanding, and responding to customers, good listening is an important skill for practitioners of Knock Your Socks Off Service. When you listen well, you:

- Figure out what your customer wants and needs.
- Prevent misunderstandings and errors.
- Gather clues about ways to improve the service you provide.
- Build long-term customer relationships.

It's important to listen actively, almost aggressively. To serve your customers well, you need to know as exactly as possible what they want, how they want it, when they want it, what they expect to pay for it, how long they expect to wait, and what else they expect. There's no need to guess—and risk being wrong. Customers are ready, willing, and able to tell you everything (or almost everything) you need to know. Listen closely to the customer for the "pain points" and move quickly to rectify the situation.

> **TIP:** Let customers know you're listening by jotting down information and ideas on how to respond—but don't dilute your focus by trying to formulate a rebuttal or argument. When you have a chance to speak, you will be able to "reflect" back your customer's key points. Reflection, even of the easy and obvious things, confirms that you have listened and understood your customer and are now ready to respond to the request, question, or problem.

Good Listeners Are Made, Not Born

People who seem to be natural listeners weren't born that way. They just started practicing a lot earlier. It's never too late to start improving because good listening is a skill that gets better as you exercise it. What's more, the listener has a powerful advantage in any conversation: While most people speak at only 125 to 150 words per minute, we can listen at up to 450 words per minute! That means we have time while listening to identify the main points the speaker is trying to make and begin to organize those points into an effective response.

Make sure you hear what the customer is trying to communicate:

1. If the information is complex, confirm your understanding by repeating it: "Okay. Let me catch up with you. You've made some important points and I want to make sure I understand. You said that you..."

2. Ask questions if you are unclear about anything: "We've talked about several options. Did you decide on the 16GB with the 3G, or the 32GB without the 3G but the special accessories package?"

3. Read back critical information—for example, the spelling of the company's name or the numbers in a street address, phone number, web site, or e-mail address—after you write it down. It ensures that you are right and assures the customer that you listened and heard.

Barriers to Effective Listening.

A wide variety of distractions can get in the way of good listening.

• *Noise.* Too much noise in your business environment causes interference. Can you easily hear customers when they speak in a normal tone of voice? Or are they drowned out by too-loud music, the general hubbub of your workplace, or the voices of your co-workers and other customers? Conversely, too little noise can also make customers uncomfortable. Customers shouldn't feel like they need to whisper in order to keep their personal information personal.

• *Interruptions.* Communication happens when two people work at it together. Have you ever tried to explain something to someone who was constantly saying, "Just a sec, gotta take this call" or looking over your shoulder to yell advice or information to a colleague? Such controllable interruptions tell customers, "You aren't important" or, "I really don't want to listen to you." And, in today's technology driven environment, the constant reminder of a new e-mail, phone message, text, or Tweet can be very distracting to you and your customer.

• *Mental Detours.* Interruptions come from inside as well as outside. When you find your thoughts drifting away to the DVD you plan to watch tonight or the fight you had with your sweetheart, or how you want to respond to the customer, that internal interruption can be every bit as destructive to good listening as working on a Wall Street trading floor. Keep the focus on your customer.

• *Technology.* Technology can hinder effective listening as much as it can help to put us in touch. For all the good service made possible by telephones, VoIP, and remote microphones in drive-up windows, it's much harder to listen to someone you can't see face-to-face or whose voice is distorted by a machine. That monitor on your desk can get in the way, as well. Rather than trying to listen to the customer and look for her account, you can simply say, "OK, Mrs. Smith, let me get your account up on my screen. . . There it is. Now, let's go over that so I can capture all the details."

• *Stereotypes.* When we label people—when we make assumptions based on what they look like, how they will behave, and what they have to say—we make it difficult to understand what they're really saying. From that false start, we fit what we later see, experience, and hear into a flawed prejudgment. And quite often we're very wrong.

• *Trigger Words and Phrases.* All of us have hot buttons that customers may inadvertently push. And once the button is pushed, listening can stop. Remember that your main concern is to listen to what your customer is trying to say, not the individual words he or she uses. What rubs you the wrong way just may be completely innocent from the customer's perspective. (And even if the customer is giving you a dig over past performance, letting it pass shows your good grace and style.)

• *Attitude.* Your attitudes color what you hear and how you respond. Defensive people evaluate everything, looking for the hidden messages. People on the offensive are too often looking for a fight, formulating oh-yes-well-let-me-tell-you-something arguments even before the other person is finished speaking. Your attitudes should help you listen, not deafen you to a customer's words.

Listening Posts

Some of the most relevant and actionable feedback comes from daily one-to-one interactions with your customers. It's in your best interest to regularly gather, summarize, and share insights, rants, or suggestions gleaned from these daily dealings with customers. Build the listening process around a simple but powerful question: What service factors do you consider most important in doing business with us?

It's also important to listen for the things that you don't hear, the things your customers aren't saying to you. If customers used to compliment you on speedy delivery, but haven't recently, perhaps your performance is slipping. If they sigh and say, "Oh, fine, I guess," when you ask them how your services measure up, you should be hearing another message loud and clear—one of a loyal customer who might be silently slipping away to the competition. Take such lukewarm responses as a cue to follow up and ask, "Are you sure there isn't any way we could serve you better?" Statistics show that rather than complain openly about a problem, many customers will simply stop doing business with you and start spending their money elsewhere.

> "People don't buy because they are made to understand. They buy because they feel understood."
>
> —Sales maxim

14

Asking Intelligent Questions

"It is better to know some of the questions than to know all of the answers."

—James Thurber

Customers are often less than articulate—or even clear in their own minds—about their wants and needs. The customer who says "I'm not quite sure," in response to your "How may I help you?" is at least being frank, and represents the feelings of a lot of customers. And it's your job to help them sort it all out.

To be successful with the unsure, unclear, or confused customer, you have to put on your detective hat. And like Sherlock Holmes, Columbo, or the criminalists on *CSI*, you have to go in search of clues. Armed with a supply of good questions, you are sure to succeed.

Three types of questions will help you in your search for clues to what the unsure customer needs from you.

Background Questions

Background questions are the introduction to your conversation. They tell you who you are talking with and allow you to pull up a customer's profile or account. They also help you evaluate whether you are the best person to help the customer, or if you should direct him or her to a different person or department.

- "Do you have an account with us?"
- "May I have your customer identification number as it appears just above the label on the back of the catalog?"
- "I have a few questions about your past medical history. First, have you had any of the following ....?"

Sometimes, customers resist background questions. "Why do you need to know that?" they ask. Or they may protest, "I gave you that information the last time I was here. Don't you keep records?" You can decrease resistance by explaining up front why you need the information. We call this tactic previewing. Here are some examples.

- "I appreciate your concern, Ms. Wilson. If you will just help me with a few questions, I'll get you connected to the best agent for your situation."
- "I need to ask you some questions about your medical history. We do this every visit to ensure that our records remain accurate and up to date."

The preview reassures your customer that you do care and that the background questions do have a purpose.

Probing Questions

Probing questions help you delve more deeply into a customer need, problem, or complaint to identify the issues involved and begin to move toward a solution. There are two basic types of questions; closed and open-ended. Closed questions are generally answered with a "Yes" or "No" or with a specific piece of information. A background question asking "What is your account number?" is a good example. Open-ended questions generally require more lengthy explanations and invite the customers into a conversation. More often than not, probing questions will be open-ended.

- "Please tell me more about your event; who will be attending, what they will be expecting, and how last year's event might be improved upon?"

- "What features are you looking for in a new bike?
- "What happened after you plugged in the DVD player?"

Remember that probing questions are a way for you to ask for information. If the answer your customer gives sounds impossible or untrue, don't dispute it. Instead, ask another probing question.

A good source of probing questions are the five W's: who, what, when, where, and why. They've served reporters well for decades.

- "Who was affected by this?"
- "What would you like to see happen next?"
- "When do you need to have the new part installed?"
- "Where did the original part break?"
- "I'd like to find out *why* this happened so we can prevent it from happening again. Please share with me your ideas?"

The exact questions you should ask will, of course, vary with the situation. And when in doubt, know you can almost always use the tried-and-true, "Please tell me more about that?"

NOTE: Be careful using "why" questions. They can sound like you are accusing the customer of something or blaming him for the problem he is reporting.

Confirmation Questions

Confirmation questions provide a "check and balance" system. They help you confirm that you've correctly understood the customer's message, and they give the customer an opportunity to add additional information or clarification.

- "That takes us through the aftercare regimen Dr. Kling prescribed. The physical exercises are the most important part and they can be challenging. Would you like to review them again?"

- "So, if we could provide you with a partial order today, or enough product to see you through Monday, will that solve your immediate problem?"

It's easy to take silence as confirmation of customer agreement. However, silence sometimes signals that the customer has given up, is frustrated, or is too embarrassed to indicate confusion. So, when your confirmation comes out as a statement, rather than as a question, it's good to ask for a response:

- "Let me make sure that I have the details right. You aren't actually moving in until the 15th, but you'll be doing work on your new home before that. Therefore, you need to have the new telephone working by the 11th, and you don't want your old telephone disconnected until the 16th. Is that right?"

TIP: If you've ever had someone fix you in the eye and ask "Do you understand?" in a slow and deliberate voice, you know how demeaning some questions can sound. Monitor your words and tone so that your confirmation doesn't communicate, "Only an idiot wouldn't understand this. Are you an idiot?"

When Good Questions Go Bad

The right question that is poorly timed or badly worded can undo all of the customer service magic you've worked so hard to create. When questions go wrong, typically one of four things has happened.

1. The question was asked at the wrong time; possibly out of sequence. There is a logic to the order in which questions should be asked. For example, it's generally easy to ask a customer's name early in the conversation, and often very awkward to do so after the two of you finish a thirty-minute conversation.

2. The customer thought you were asking about something he believes you should know. Use the preview technique to explain why you need to ask.

- "I know that Hector has your number, but could I take it down again for quick reference?"

3. The customer feels you are asking too many questions. Make your questions count, for you and for your customer.

- "How are you today? Are you the lady of the house? Am I catching you at a good time? Would you be willing to answer a few questions for the study we're doing?"

4. The question feels too personal. What's personal and what's just conversation will vary from person to person. If you're asking because you're curious, it may be better not to. If you're asking because you need the information, use the preview technique to explain why before you ask.

- "In order for us to build the best financial plan for you, I'll need to ask you some important questions about your personal finances. Of course, all the information we work with today will remain confidential. Do you have any questions before we begin?"

"Only when you begin to ask the right questions do you begin to find the right answers."

—Dorothy Leeds
Smart Questions: A New Strategy for Successful Managers

15

Winning Words and Soothing Phrases

"Politeness goes far, yet costs nothing."
—Samuel Smiles
Nineteenth-century popular writer

"Oh yeah?! Sticks and stones may break my bones, but words will never hurt me." Sound familiar? As children, we recited those words many times. They were our self-defense in the very situations where we learned that words did hurt—emotionally, if not physically. And many of us carry memories that remind us that the pain words inflict can be more devastating than any bruise or broken arm.

Words are just as powerful to adults. We are capable of bruising or soothing our customers with words; it all depends on how we use them. The service professional who can use words well gains a distinct advantage in the service transaction.

Forbidden Phrases

Some words, alone or in combination, create immediate negative images. Nancy Friedman, a customer service and telephone skills consultant known to many by her business persona, "The Telephone Doctor,"™ advocates a ban on what she calls Five Forbidden Phrases—five responses that, intentionally or unintentionally, can drive your customers right up the wall in anger or frustration. They are listed here in Table 15-1, with her suggested alternatives:

Table 15-1.

Forbidden Phrase	Use Instead
I don't know.	"Gee, that's a good question. Let me check and find out."
We can't do that.	"Boy that's a tough one. Let's see what we can do." Then find an alternative solution.
You'll have to...	Soften the request with phrases like, I'd like to suggest," or "Here's how we can help you with that," or "The next time that happens, here's what you can do."
Hang on a second: I'll be right back.	"It may take me two or three minutes (or however long it will really take) to get that. Are you able to hold/wait while I check?"
"No" when used at the beginning of any sentence.	If you think before you speak, you can turn every negative answer into a positive response, "We aren't able to refund your money, but we can replace the product at no charge."

While those five phrases are sure to raise customer ire, they aren't the only ones. Which ones not on the list above would rile you as a customer?

TIP: Create your own list of Do Say and Don't Say words and phrases. Use the list from Table 15-2 to get started. You'll be able to add many more using your own experience and the insight of co-workers. What words and phrases are guaranteed to bring a smile to your customer's face? Which ones create a frown? Add to it from your

experiences as a customer and as a service professional. (Note: All of the examples below come
from real life situations.)

The Message Behind the Words

Every Knock Your Socks Off Service professional has times
when something said in all sincerity or innocence to a customer, something that sounds reasonable and rational to you,
causes the customer to explode with anger. It's not the intent of
your words to create customer anger, but it is the effect. As you
learn to notice some of the common words and phrases that provoke these undesirable responses, you'll find yourself becoming more successful at avoiding or defusing such situations.

Table 15-2.

Don't Say	Do Say
"She went to get another candy bar."	"She's not available right now."
"Are we through yet?"	"Will there be anything else?"
"No problem."	"It will be my pleasure. Or, I'd be happy to."
"Honey" or "Buddy" or "Lady"	"The customer's name (the way he or she wishes it to be used)."
"Well, that's not really my concern."	"It's clear that you are frustrated."
"Yeah, yeah, I'll get to it."	"I'll take care of that for you personally."
"You've got the wrong department."	"I handle small appliances. Let me transfer you to the department that I am confident can help you."
"That's not my job."	"I usually don't handle that area, but I know who can help you. Let me see if she's available."
"It's over there (and point)."	"Let me walk you over there" or "Do you see the blue sign? It's directly to the left of that."

One of the most common negative messages we can send to customers, whether intended or not, is, "I think you're stupid." We send that message when we use phrases like, "Do you understand?" with that certain tone of voice, or when we begin talking to a customer as if we are addressing a four-year-old (even though the customer's behavior may be straight out of preschool). If four-year-olds don't appreciate being talked down to, why should adult customers find it enjoyable or satisfying?

A cable TV technician described a helpful technique to ensure understanding without demeaning the customer in the *Customer Connection Newsletter*. The technicians needed to make sure the customer on the phone was starting from the right point:

> "Before I can help [a subscriber] with a problem, it's important for me to confirm that the set is tuned in to the right channel. . . . When I ask 'Is the TV tuned to channel 3?' the customer answers 'Yes' automatically . . . and I'm uncomfortable saying 'Please go and check.' So now I say, 'Will you please go to the TV set and turn it to channel 5. Wait for ten seconds then turn it back to channel 3. Then come back and tell me what happened.' This gets the action I need without having to challenge the customer's word."

Scripting the Panic Away

Telemarketers, those people who call you at dinner to sell you things, have for years used scripts; prewritten conversations intended to help them put their best foot forward.

Service people are often reluctant to use scripts for fear that they would sound robotic or mechanical in their interactions with customers. And that can happen. But it doesn't have to.

Service consultant Gail Boylan, former chief nurse at Baptist Health Group in Pensacola, Florida, used to feel the same way: "I hated the idea of scripting. It seemed like an insult to people's intelligence." Nonetheless, encouraged by what she

saw in an award-winning hospital in Chicago, she and her colleagues wrote some simple scripts—phrases everyone could
use with patients—that had a dramatic effect on customer perceptions of service and caring.

One group of nurses came up with the idea of saying, "I'm
closing this curtain to help protect your privacy," when cur-
taining off a patient's bed. Patients began remarking on how
caring and concerned the staff was.

Before leaving a patient's room, cleaning staff, nurses'
aides, and maintenance people began saying, "Is there anything else I can do for you: I have the time right now to help
you." Comments about how considerate the staff was were
suddenly heard all over the hospital. Equally important, the
number of nonmedical calls from patients to the nursing sta-
tions decreased by 40 percent.

Security personnel at airports have their own scripts as
well. A simple "thanks for your patience" as customers are
asked to remove their shoes or pull laptops out of carrying
cases goes a long way toward creating goodwill and showing
concern for the inconveniences of today's airplane travel.

Service scripts work best when:

- They are short and easy to remember.
- They are developed around issues that are important to
  customers.
- People are free to paraphrase them, or put them into
  their own words so they don't sound rote or mechanical.

The best service scripts? That's easy. Those are the ones
you and your colleagues sit down and write for yourselves.

"Man does not live by words alone, despite the
fact that sometimes he has to eat them."

—Adlai Stevenson
Lawyer and politician

16

Facts for
Face-to-Face

"I solemnly promise and declare that for every customer that comes within ten feet of me, I will smile, look
them in the eye and greet them, so help me Sam."

—Employee pledge, Wal-Mart stores

The words we speak, hear, or read are only a small part of the
way we communicate with one another. Experts suggest that
in face-to-face situations, at least 70 percent of what is com-
municated is done without speaking a word. This is called
nonverbal communication.

What is nonverbal communication? It's everything we
don't say—our body language, how we act and react, and what
we show to others when we are with them. There are nine basic dimensions of nonverbal communication. Knock Your
Socks Off Service professionals are keenly aware of each.

1. *Proximity.* Carry on a conversation with a co-worker
while standing about an arm's length apart. After a few minutes, move forward until your noses are about six inches apart.
Feel uncomfortable? Most North Americans will. The same
will be true if you're standing six feet apart. "Comfort zones"
vary from culture to culture. Most North Americans prefer to
maintain a distance of between a foot and a half and two feet.
Europeans, except for the English, tend to be comfortable
standing closer. The same goes for most South Americans.

2. *Eye Contact.* Making eye contact acknowledges that you see your customers as individuals and that you are paying attention. There's a balance to be struck here: People who don't make eye contact in the American culture are considered shifty or even dishonest, but staring can make your customers uncomfortable, too. And eye contact in Europe, Asia, the Middle East, Mexico, and South America is governed by specific cultural rules (for more tips on serving customers from other cultures, see Chapter 18). A good rule to follow is to give as much as you get.

3. *Silence.* You can and do communicate even when you're saying nothing. Remaining silent while your customers are talking is a basic courtesy, and nodding tells them you're listening and understanding what you hear. Prolonged silence, however, can leave customers concerned that either you did not hear them or that you disagree with what they said. An occasional "uh huh" or "I see" tells them you're still listening without interrupting.

4. *Gestures.* Closed gestures such as tightly crossed arms, hands tucked deep in pockets or clenched fists create nonverbal barriers. Open gestures invite people into our space and say we're comfortable having them near us. Many of our gestures are unconscious (some people cross their arms when the room is cold, for example), so make a point of thinking about what you're doing nonverbally when you deal with customers.

5. *Posture.* "Stand up straight," your mother always said, and she was right. Good physical posture conveys confidence and competence. Leaning in slightly when customers are talking says you think what they are saying is important and interesting.

6. *Facial Expression.* We all know the cues: A raised eyebrow communicates surprise; a wink indicates sly agreement or alliance; tightly set lips, opposition; a wide open smile, friendliness. Your face communicates, even when your voice doesn't.

7. *Physical Contact.* What is and is not appropriate today varies greatly with the situation and the people involved.

A handshake is customary, but placing a hand on another person's arm or an arm over someone's shoulder can be a very personal act. The rule of thumb is "less is best" in most professional situations.

8. *Smell.* This is perhaps the least understood of our senses, but an important one in service work that involves getting close to customers. Be just as careful with strong perfumes and colognes—some customers may be sensitive or allergic—as you are of the natural odors they are used to cover up. Be aware, too, that at a time when fewer adults smoke, the lingering smell of tobacco can be offensive.

9. *Overall Appearance.* Just as in a theatrical performance, you have to look your part. Whether your costume is a three-piece suit or blue coveralls depends on the job you do, what you want to communicate to customers, and especially what your customers expect to see. Whatever the case, one thing will always be true of your physical appearance: Cleanliness and neatness communicate competence. (Messy people may be just as competent as neat people, but they will have to work a lot harder to prove it to the customer!)

Nonverbal Cues

The flip side of nonverbal communication is knowing how to read the nonverbal cues of your customers. Almost everyone can look at other people and read their obvious body language. We know when others are happy or sad, calm, or upset.

> **TIP:** Sometimes the nonverbal messages we send are more powerful, more persuasive, and more revealing than the words we speak. When our nonverbal signals send a different message than our words, our customers can become confused, disoriented, or skeptical of our motives, actions, and interest in serving their needs. A significant part of your success as a service professional will come from how you manage your face-to-face, nonverbal communications.

What makes one person appear so at ease in social situations or in dealing with customers while others seem uncomfortable or inept? Research suggests that the difference may lie in what we do with what we know. Socially adept individuals more readily accept and act on the body language signals they see. Others plow blindly ahead, unmindful of the confused looks that say, "Please stop and explain that again."

Customers may not always speak up when they feel uncomfortable or confused or frustrated. But if you "listen" for the unspoken messages, you pick up the nonverbal cues as well as the audible ones. Use them effectively and they'll help you meet and exceed your customer's needs and expectations.

"Perception is the key to nonverbal success."

—Sales training axiom

17

Tips for Telephone Talk

"If I pick up a ringing phone, I accept the responsibility to ensure the caller is satisfied, no matter what the issue."

—Michael Ramundo
The Complete Idiot's Guide to Motivating People

Using the telephone requires you to be more aware of your voice than at any other time. Customers cannot hear your facial expressions or see your nonverbal clues—like shrugs or hand gestures. They do form a mental picture of you based on the tone and quality of your voice. Your mood—smiling and happy or tight-lipped and angry—often comes through. That's why, before you ever pick up a telephone or put on a headset, you should take a moment to be sure that you are mentally prepared to deal with the customer on the other end. A pleasant phone voice takes practice. This Telephone Style Checklist (see Table 17-1) can help you assess your phone style. After all, speaking in well-modulated, pleasant tones is a learned talent.

TIP: Tape record yourself talking on the phone, then ask an honest friend or your boss to evaluate your vocal quality. Better yet, have someone tape you from the listener's end so you can listen to how you sound to your customers.

Table 17-1.

TELEPHONE STYLE CHECKLIST		
Vocal Quality	Yes	No
Voice is easy to hear without being too loud.	☐	☐
Words are clearly articulated.	☐	☐
Pacing is good—neither too slow nor too fast.	☐	☐
Vocal tone is pleasant—neither grating nor nasal.	☐	☐
Energy level shows interest and enthusiasm.	☐	☐
Phone Techniques		
Phone is answered quickly—on the second or third ring.	☐	☐
Caller is greeted courteously.	☐	☐
Representative identifies self to caller.	☐	☐
Transfers are handled professionally.	☐	☐
Messages taken are complete and accurate.	☐	☐

WARNING: If you have never heard your recorded voice before, you will be surprised at the way you sound. Don't let it bother you: We all sound strange to ourselves on tape.

Telephone Etiquette: A Quick Review

Professional telephone talk involves four basic customer-sensitive processes. Knowing and following them will ensure that your customers feel you are really taking care of them.

Answering the Phone

The ringing of a telephone is one of the most insistent sounds in the world. (Just try to let your phone ring without answering it. Most people can't.) When a customer calls and no one answers, or the line is busy, or it rings fifteen times before someone picks it up, it's like telling the customer "I'm sorry, but you will have to take your money and leave the store. We are very busy here and we just don't have time to help you. Please go shop somewhere else. And thank you for trying to do business with us." Set a standard for yourself (two or three rings, for example) and try to meet it every time.

When you answer the phone, remember that your customer can hear you from the moment the handset leaves the cradle or the second your headset is activated. You wouldn't want your customer to be greeted with, (distant voice) "So, I told her a thing or two... (direct voice) Oh, hello."

> **WINNING PHRASE:** "Hello, you've reached Acme Inc. This is Monica. How may I help you?" The best greetings contain three elements. First, a greeting, like "Hello" or "Good morning." Because some phone systems cut off the first word, the greeting protects the second element, the identification statement. Crime Stopper's Hint: Practice saying your identification statement slowly. Too often the identification is so rushed, the caller doesn't know who he or she has reached, "helloAcmeAcresHow-MayIHelpYou" is not one word – it just sounds like it when delivered by a bored service rep.

Entering Information

Frequently, customer calls require that you look up information or enter information into a computer system. When you are doing that face-to-face the customer sees you working away and almost automatically exercises patience and paces the information flow accordingly.

Over the phone, the customer can't see your fingers flying across the keyboard or mouse pad. To give yourself the time you need to bring up the customer's account, find the information the customer needs or to enter the customer's data, subtly cue the customer by describing what you are doing. Phrases like:

> "Ok, Mrs. Smith, let me get your account up on my screen. . . Here we are. OK. I see here you placed that order on the 15th. . . ."

And

> "Let me get that entered into my computer here. OK, that's 35185 Virginia Drive, Sycamore, s-y-c-a-m-o-r-e, Indiana."

Working aloud—talking as you are entering customer information or bringing up her account—lets the customer know what you are doing and assures her that you haven't put her on hold and walked off to get coffee.

CAUTION: Don't make small talk with customers about the slow speed of your computer system. That suggests your company is out of date and raises doubts about your reliability.

Putting a Caller on Hold

Sometimes callers have to be put on hold. You may need to answer a second line, you may need to leave your desk to get a piece of information, or you may just need a moment to regroup while handling a particularly volatile caller.

Whatever the circumstances, never put a caller on hold without first asking permission—"May I put you on hold?" or, "Are you able to hold, please?" And the question means nothing if you don't wait for the answer. Yes, it takes a moment longer. But it is well worth it for the positive impression

it creates. And yes, you risk hearing, "No, you may not." Accept that and either reprioritize things or take the caller's number and call back as quickly as possible.

The caller who doesn't want to hold is not necessarily being pushy. Recently, a good friend of ours phoned her doctor's office. Because the receptionist knew her, she assumed she could just park her on hold with an "Oh, Nancy, hang on a minute" while she handled another call. That assumption was almost fatal. Nancy had just crawled to the phone after suffering a major medical problem.

> **WINNING PHRASE:** When you are juggling multiple calls, and need to put nonemergency calls on hold, use "Are you able to hold?" instead of "May I put you on hold?" Customers will often respond yes to the "Are you able" question, even when holding is not what they prefer to do.

Her case is a rare one, to be sure, but callers may have other legitimate reasons for not wanting to hold. Remember that Knock Your Socks Off Service is delivered individually to match what each customer needs and expects.

> **WINNING PHRASE:** "May I have your phone number for quick reference?" Customers sometimes resent leaving their phone numbers—"He has it. After

all, I'm returning his call." The "for quick reference"
phrase will help you bypass that negative response
and take a complete message.

Taking Messages

Good messages are accurate and complete. If you're not
transferring callers into voice mail, be sure to get their full
name, company name, and phone number. "Tell her Bill
called" only works if the person the message is intended for
knows only one Bill. To make sure you have the correct
spelling of the caller's name and an accurate phone number,
read it back. The date and time of the message is also important. Finally, be sure to put your own name on the message;
if there is any question, the message recipient will be able to
ask you for clarification.

Transferring Calls

Customers hate to be passed from pillar to post to Pammy to
Paul and back again. Whenever possible, don't do it. Help the
caller yourself or take a message and have the appropriate
person return the call. When you do have to transfer a call, be
sure to give the name and phone number of the person who
will help them. This way, if there is any problem with the
switch, the caller will be able to get back to the right person.
And if you can, stay on the line to be sure the transfer goes
smoothly.

> **WINNING PHRASE:** "Jose, I'm transferring a call
> from Mr. Polasky to you. He needs an update on
> his account." Let the person you are transferring
> the call to know who is on the line and why you're
> transferring the call. One caution: Always talk
> about the caller in respectful terms—never as-
> sume your customer can't hear you simply
> because he or she is supposed to be on hold dur-
> ing the transfer.

Voice Mail and Caller ID

Voice mail is both the biggest boon and the biggest bane of
modern business. We have a real love/hate relationship with
this tool. To use voice mail in the best possible way, remember these guidelines:

- Voice mail is not a substitute for, but rather a supple-
  ment to, real-time phone communication. When you
  have the option, always try to talk directly to a customer rather than leave a message or series of messages.
- Caller ID is not an excuse to check to see who is calling
  and then decide whether or not to take the call. Your
  internal customers are every bit as important as the external customer.
- Change your message frequently, providing up-to-date
  information about whether or not you are in, when you
  will pick up and return messages, and who the caller
  might contact if her request can't wait.
- Tell callers what information to leave. Some systems
  automatically "tag" incoming messages with the date
  and time. If your system doesn't, you may need to remind callers to provide that information.
- Let your callers know how to use your system. "To indicate that your message is urgent, press 1." Or, "In the
  future, you may skip this message by pressing the
  pound key."
- Call your voice mail periodically to ensure that the
  message is clear and that the voice mail system is working properly. Systems can break down, fill up, and
  malfunction.
- Return messages promptly. Many customer service reps
  follow the sundown rule: Return all calls within the
  same day, preferably within a few hours of receiving
  them.
- When you leave a voice message for someone, be sure
  to state your name and phone number twice—once at
  the beginning of your message and once at the end.
  And, be sure to state your phone number slowly—
  pretend you're writing it down as you say it.

Taking full advantage of the benefits of telephone talk requires that you understand and can easily use the features on your telephone system. If you're using a new voice-over-Internet protocol (VOIP) phone system, for example, and haven't mastered all of the technology's features, make sure you ask for assistance so you're not forced to "practice" with live customers.

Teleconferencing

Whether you are a participant in a teleconference—more than two people connected to a single phone conversation—or are simply making the connection for the meeting, there are some important protocols to remember.

1. Once the time and date for the teleconference is set, make sure everyone who will be participating has the dial-in instructions and meeting time. Double-check that information: phone and e-mail it to the participants.

> **TIP:** If the teleconference is scheduled for more than seven days in the future, be sure to e-mail participants a reminder the afternoon before the teleconference—if it is an A.M. teleconference—or the morning of the teleconference if it is a noon or afternoon call. And if the teleconference crosses time zones, which they usually do, specify the start time by time zone. For instance: If the teleconference is being set up by a person in Chicago, and all the participants will be from the United States, your notes to participants should specify central time zone: "The conference call will begin at 10:00 A.M. CT."

2. Introductions are important for making the most of conference call time and to avoid confusion. If you are the conference call originator, be the first one to connect and have a printed list of participants in front of you. As you hear people joining the call, ask them to identify themselves:

"I believe someone just joined us. This is Sara from ABC Widget. Could you identify yourself?" And as others join, let them know who is already on the line. For instance: "Thank you for joining us. Bill Gras and Mary Hadder are also with us. Bill is vice president of the color widget division and Mary is director of customer service. Bill and Mary, could you say hello?"

> **TIP:** Think of a teleconference as a meeting in a large windowless room during a power outage. Your job is to help everyone find a seat and get comfortable with the other participants.

3. Once everyone is in—online—take a few seconds to establish the ground rules. Here are two:

- If there are more than four people in the meeting, people should be asked to identify themselves when they speak, as in: "This is Sara. I couldn't agree with you more, Bill. And I'd like to add. . ."
- If there is an agenda ask participants to have it in front of them.

4. Review assignments and follow-up activities before everyone hangs up and the conference ends. Follow up with an e-mail confirming everyone's commitments and assignments.

5. If this is a client conference, do not review the meeting with your colleagues on the conference line. Hang up and call everyone back, or, if you all work in the same facility, meet face to face. Never postmortem a tele-meeting on the conference line. You cannot be sure everyone has hung up. Avoid the potential embarrassment of saying something you wouldn't want the client to hear while they are still on the line!

> "When you answer the phone, your store's image is on the line."
>
> —Headline
> *Video Business* magazine

18

It's a Small World:

Culturally Sensitive Service

"The single greatest barrier to business success is the one erected by culture."

—Edward Hall,
cross-cultural communications expert

It can be tough enough to meet the demands and soothe the frustrations of customers who share the same language, use the same jargon, or have the same business customs that you do. Magnify that service challenge with customers who haven't yet mastered your mother tongue, who come from cultures with often-mystifying service expectations, or who can be offended by communication practices you take for granted, and the potential for customer service breakdowns grows exponentially.

Whether based in New York, Bangalore, or Manila, you're likely dealing each day with customers from more cultures and countries than ever before. The world is shrinking, and serving a multicultural customer base requires a new understanding of the unique values, expectations, and cultural norms people from other parts of the world bring to a service interaction.

Be too direct in your communications or use too much eye contact with certain customers from the Pacific Rim and it can be perceived as rude service. Be too chatty with callers

from Germany—or use a first name before invited to do so—
and they may be put off by the informality. Speak with a
hard-to-decipher accent when fielding calls from Western customers in overseas call centers and it may trigger a flurry of
complaints by unhappy clients to top executives. Ask customers from Japan whether they're satisfied with how you
handled a service problem and the "yes" you hear in response
may not signal agreement but rather a desire to avoid con-
frontation and maintain harmony.

Missteps in communicating across cultures can do more
than momentarily upset customers—they can also cost your
company untold dollars in missed sales, derail important
relationship-building opportunities, and lead to costly client
turnover.

Delivering Globally Friendly Service

You can't, of course, expect to learn all of the cultural quirks,
body language booby traps, or service preferences of customers from every culture you might do business with. Nor
does stereotyping aid your cause. Entering service encounters
with too many preconceived notions about those from other
cultures and failing to adapt your approach for individual

differences means you're likely to leave plenty of offended customers in your wake.

That said, cultural researchers have identified behavioral norms, values, and belief systems of many cultures around the world that can be helpful to know in advance of service interactions. We've listed some here to help you navigate the intercultural speed bumps that can arise in today's global marketplace, along with tips for making it easier for nonnative speakers of your language to do business with you.

- **Respect is the universal language of service.** Customers from other cultures may forgive you for not knowing all the technical specifications of a product or the details of your latest advertised special, but the forgiveness usually ends if you are impatient with their imperfect English, strong accents, or difficult-to-pronounce names. Being patient, respecting differences, and allowing customers to be heard can help bridge even the widest cultural gulf.

"The underlying premise to delivering quality service in any culture is that you respect the individual customer," says Cynthia Messer, an associate professor and coordinator of the University of Minnesota Tourism Center's *At Your Service* training program, which teaches organizations how to better serve a multicultural customer base.

- **Simplify and clarify language with nonnative speakers.** When serving customers still learning your native tongue, it pays to speak more deliberately, limit your use of potentially confusing synonyms or acronyms, and make clear transitions between thoughts. In this case, the more bland your language the better. Customers learning English as a second language, for example, can get confused by first talking about "benefits" and later referring to them as "advantages."

Speaking at a slower rate—but not so slow as to seem condescending—and using more pauses also aids comprehension. But avoid the temptation to turn up the volume. While that might work with your deaf Uncle Al, it will just annoy or offend multicultural customers.

Roger Axtell, author of the bestselling book *Essential Do's and Taboos: The Complete Guide to International Business Travel* (John Wiley and Sons, 2007), says the technique of "echoing" can help ensure nonnative speakers understand what you're saying. For example, you might say, "Sometimes I speak too fast. Maybe it would be good to stop and have you review, in your words, what we've talked about so far."

- **Be conscious of your "slanguage."** Americans use more figures of speech, slang, sports metaphors, and business buzzwords than perhaps any other nation on the planet. Using idioms like "run it up the flagpole," or "flying by the seat of our pants" with customers unfamiliar with such terms can leave them wondering what planet you've beamed down from.

While you can't eliminate all of these phrases, you can become more conscious of using them and make sure you're being understood. And if you're working in a call center outside of the United States or England but dealing primarily with U.S- or U.K-based customers, it helps to familiarize yourself with the most commonly used figures of speech in those countries. Two good resources are the *Amerispeak* web site (www.rootsweb.com/~genepool/amerispeak.htm), which explains many common American idioms and the *Dictionary of*

Slang in the United Kingdom (www.peevish.co.uk/slang), the equivalent for potentially confusing British sayings.

Improving Your Cross-Cultural IQ

Understanding the forces that shape the beliefs, behaviors, and biases of other cultures can help you avoid surprises and misunderstandings in cross-cultural service situations. Here are a few cultural practices and belief systems found around the globe that may differ from your own:

- **A low tolerance for uncertainty.** Customers in countries like Japan, China, parts of Latin America, Germany, and Greece tend to be less comfortable with ambiguity than Americans are. Dutch professor and cultural researcher Geert Hofstede called this phenomenon *uncertainty avoidance*, defining it as "the extent to which members of a culture feel threatened by uncertain or unknown situations."

Customers from these cultures often strive to eliminate uncertainties and expect absolute truths. In service situations, be aware that these customers may prefer highly detailed instructions rather than broad guidelines, particularly in problem-solving scenarios. When in doubt, don't assume— ask what approach customers would prefer.

- **High-context and low-context cultures**. High-context cultures depend more on nonverbal or indirect communication methods to get their points across. In high-context countries, such as Mexico and Japan, facial expressions or body language are often more highly valued than words themselves. In low-context cultures, such as the United States, Australia, and Germany, the best and most trusted form of communication is usually considered the spoken word.

- **Personalization isn't a universal need.** As members of a highly individualistic culture, American customers like to feel they're special, and U.S. service workers are often taught to "personalize" interactions by using customers' first names, making note of previous buying preferences or encouraging special orders.

But this craving to feel unique isn't universal, especially in "collectivist" or more group-oriented cultures. In a study detailed in *The Journal of Marketing Theory and Practice*, researcher Kathryn Winsted examined the service expectations of customers in Japan and the United States in medical and restaurant settings. Among the biggest differences she found was the role that personalized service played in customer satisfaction. One member of a Japanese focus group expressed amazement, for example, that when she once had to go to the hospital by ambulance in the United States, the emergency technicians kept using her name throughout the trip. All focus group participants agreed that would never happen in Japan; in such group-oriented cultures personalizing service for one person can be considered an affront to another.

- **Time isn't money everywhere on the planet.** While customers from the United States, England, or Germany might have little patience for chitchat during a service encounter, many in Italy, France, or the Middle East might be downright offended without sufficient getting-to-know-you conversation before moving on to business.

Read customer cues carefully and adjust your approach based on what you see, hear, or feel. Continue the "how's the weather?" discussion until the customer initiates the business part of the interaction. If they're taking too long to get down to business, simply say, "It's been nice chatting with you, now what can I help you with today?"

> "Culture is more often a source of conflict than of synergy. Cultural differences are a nuisance at best and often a disaster."
>
> —Dr. Geert Hofstede

19
The Generational Divide:
Serving Age-Diverse Customers

"I couldn't care less how friendly they are or whether they call me 'Mr.' Just fix my problem right the first time and forget about buttering me up."
— 30-something customer overheard on his lunch break talking about a computer problem.

To celebrate their wedding anniversary, a 60-something Mid-western couple chose a popular new restaurant in their small town for dinner. Upon being seated they were met with a warm greeting by their server, who congratulated them on their anniversary and appeared to set a good tone for their special evening.

But then she handed each of them a menu, pulled up a chair, sat down and proceeded to review the menu and the daily specials. While some customers may have been touched by the gesture, the couple grew uncomfortable and a little peeved. To their way of thinking, the casual, elbow-to-elbow approach was disrespectful. After all, they hadn't invited her to sit with them and however well-intended, the action violated an unspoken boundary between server and customer.

So, Wally and Bev, what are my new best friends going to have for dinner?

The ability to "get inside the heads" of customers is essential to delivering memorable service, and never more so than when serving customers from different generations. Whether they're part of the World War II era, Baby Boomers, Generation Xers, Millennial's, or the soon-to-be-monikered generation to follow, each age group has its own distinct definition of good service. A couple in their 20s, for example, might have welcomed or even been quietly amused by the server's breezy attitude and attempt to add a personal touch to the anniversary dining experience. But for those of an older generation, the lack of formality and deference to roles felt unsettling and inappropriate.

Serving the Generational Melting Pot

Ensuring customers of various ages and eras receive service "their way" starts with understanding the distinct characteristics, attitudes, and life-shaping events that define them. To help you with that task we've created profiles of four distinct generational segments and listed some of the service preferences for each group. These "likes and dislikes" are designed as guidelines, not set-in-stone rules. As with all things in life there'll be exceptions to every rule, so you'll want to stay flexible and adapt your approach to perceived variations in each generation.* The profiles reflect more than a decade of our own research, as well as the findings of Claire Raines, with whom we collaborated on the book *Generations at Work: AMACOM, 2000.*

Veterans are customers born between 1922 and 1943, or just prior to World War II. These are your clients in their late 60s through their 80s.

Some defining characteristics of Veterans are:

- A desire for consistency, conformity, and stability.
- Direct communication style.
- Preference for logical and pragmatic discussion or approaches, rather than that driven by emotion.
- Tend to be loyal consumers, particularly to U.S.-made products or services.

Tips for Serving Veterans:

- Don't rush things. Veterans don't like to be pushed for decisions or to feel like transactions are moving too quickly. Where possible, use a relaxed pace that allows them to think through options and feel comfortable with outcomes.
- Establish rapport by being respectful—the old-fashioned way. That means saying "please," "thank you" "sir," and "ma'am" more than you might with other generations.
- Be formal. Veterans often get uneasy with too much chumminess or overly casual approaches in service situations. Try to create a respectful "distance" with them—until invited to behave otherwise.

Baby Boomers were born between 1943 and 1960, making them one of the largest generations in U.S. history. These are the bulk of your middle-aged customers, in their 50s through their late 60s.

---

* Some of our generational "bookend" birth dates vary from standards typically used by demographers. For example, most define the Baby Boom as those born between 1946 and 1964. We opted to include those born from 1943–1946 as well because our research shows they share most of the values and views of those born a few years later. Ditto for Generation X, which we date starting from 1960 rather than the traditional 1965.

Here are some traits that define Boomers:

- Tend to be optimistic, seeing the world in terms of infinite possibility.
- Strong sense of individuality, with many accustomed to being in the spotlight.
- Value personalized treatment.
- Proponents of collaborating and cooperating with others to achieve goals.

Tips for Serving Boomers:

• Be personable, especially in your greeting. While your Boomer customers may not feel like taking the time to "visit," they will appreciate the warmth of a hearty greeting.

• If you know the customer's name, use it. Many Boomers like to be "known" and enjoy the personalization. But don't go overboard; using names too frequently will come across as smarmy or artificial.

• If customers are regulars, give them something extra from time to time to recognize their loyalty. In deciding who to do business with, Boomers often look for organizations that have employees who aren't just competent or efficient, but who seem to care about customers and see customer service work as their calling. Small acts that show them you care can go a long way.

Generation Xers, born between 1960 and 1980, are the much-maligned (often unjustly so) generation in their 30's to 50's.

Some character traits of Generations Xers:

- They are technologically savvy, clever, and resourceful.
- Tend to be skeptical, "prove it to me" sorts.
- Self-reliant and independent. Many have a "survivor" mentality and cope better with change than other generations.
- Strong need for flexibility and feedback, coupled with a dislike for close supervision.

Tips for Serving Generation X:

- Be efficient and to the point. Competence is far more important to most Xers than having an upbeat or cheerful attitude. To them, a grumpy refund beats a smiling, "we're so sorry we can't take that back" almost every time.
- Be prepared to field questions. Gen Xers are curious types who like to nail down the details, so make sure you know your stuff and can provide correct facts or figures about products or services when asked.
- Don't oversell products or solutions. Xers have finely tuned "crap detectors" and are sensitive to anything that reeks of the hard-sell or pure marketing spin. If possible, cite specific examples of how your products or services have helped customers solve problems or quote independent research that compares your organization favorably against competitors.

Millennials are those born between 1980 and 2000 making them tweens to early 30's. This group also is known as Echo Boomers, Generation Y, or Nexters.

Millennials' defining characteristics:

- Sociable, optimistic but practical, tolerant of individual differences. Generally not as sarcastic as Gen Xers, and more trusting of authority.
- Achievement- and goal-oriented. Believe in hard work and sacrificing personal pleasure for the common good.

- Thanks to doting Boomer parents, among the smartest and healthiest generation on the planet. Many have been catered to since they were tots.
- First generation to grow up in the era of digital media.

Tips for Serving Millennials:

- Be respectful. No one likes to be talked down to just because they're young. Beware of condescending tones or of passing off common sense as "insider wisdom." Millennials like to feel like equals.
- Use a quick pace. Millennials are used to having needs met "yesterday" and often find overly deliberate people or processes taxing.
- Take pains not to confuse them with Generation Xers. While most generations don't like to be mistaken for others, Millennials in particular chafe at being lumped together with Generation Xers, finding them too edgy or cynical for their tastes.

Generational Service Worksheet

Answering these questions can help you deliver more effective service to the different generations in your own organization:

- Which generation (or generations) are most of your customers from?
- When it comes to customer service, how do you think most of them want to be treated?
- What are three specific things you might do to improve service for your most dominant (largest) generational group?
- Is there another generation you'd like to target for improved service? How might you enhance or modify service in ways that would better appeal to this group?

"Trends wrought by generational differences are causing business upheavals, bringing new categories of work into being at warp speed and causing old ones to shrink and disappear."

—Yankelovich Partners

III

Communicating Knock Your Socks Off Service

Service-savvy organizations know that each customer touch-point, whether conducting a mundane transaction or handling a potentially catastrophic problem, is a Moment of Truth that should be approached with the same forethought and care. But in today's über-networked environment, one wrong move and your indifferent or dismissive treatment of any customer can be retold across the web or can attract millions of hits on YouTube. Delivering Knock Your Socks Off Service means ensuring that regardless of who customers come into contact with in your organization, and no matter how many of your associates play a role in meeting their needs, they feel served by a company "rowing together as one" in pursuit of their satisfaction.

This kind of "seamless" service requires understanding how your job fits into the bigger picture of the customer's experience and knowing that if things go wrong at your link in the chain it can have dramatic consequences for customer loyalty. It requires constant and regular communication. It means serving your internal partners—those co-workers who depend on you for timely, competent work to do their jobs—with the same diligence and care that you provide external customers.

Where thorough communication and seamless service exist, a customer's problem or request becomes the responsibility of anyone in the organization who comes into contact with him.

20

Co-Workers
as Partners:

Communicating
Across Functions

"Where does my work go?"

"Who is my work important to?"

—Dun & Bradstreet

We've all been there. A customer calls your company's 800 number, isn't sure where to go in the menu, presses a number and is suddenly beamed into your world—even though he needs Brad in billing in another state. Maybe you're working the floor of a cavernous home improvement store and a persistent customer approaches while you're in the midst of serving someone else, asking where to find a lighting fixture located in another time zone on the opposite side of the store. Or perhaps you're sweating blood trying to make a project deadline when an associate from sales barges breathlessly into your cubicle and pleads for copies of the first-quarter sales figures to include in tomorrow's client presentation.

Whether the source is co-workers or wayward customers, it's easy to view these requests as interruptions to your real work or as responsibilities that fall outside the realm of your normal job duties. But the reality is when customer satisfaction is at stake—when there's a clear opportunity to knock someone's socks off—it's important to do what's needed in the moment to ensure that external customers or work associates walk away with their needs met.

Regardless of whether they're in a cubicle just down the hall, across the city, or in another state or country, if they depend on you and the work you do to complete their own work, it's just as important to serve co-workers' needs as it is your external customer's needs. When you help associates in your company, you help the organization and its customers succeed.

We're not, of course, talking about dropping everything to help associates who make frivolous or consistently unreasonable requests. You need to be able to separate essential from nonessential requests and tasks, then assign higher priority and focus to the former. We're also not suggesting that you do others' work for them or assume a subservient role to your associates.

The term *internal customer* is often used to describe relationships with co-workers, but we believe it's more appropriate to think of them as *partners*. Chip Bell, founder of the Chip Bell Group in Dallas, Texas, says the word "customer" implies deference to others, while partnerships are about equality. When you are someone else's customer, it suggests—rightly or wrongly—that one of the two parties is in charge and that someone may be in a "one-down" position.

"Serving customers suggests their needs take precedence over ours," Bell says. "While a service orientation is essential to all relationships, it can help avoid power struggles if colleagues are thought of as equal partners rather than as customers."

Know Your Organizational Chart

To help customers with requests or problems that go beyond your area of expertise, or to aid those lost souls who inadvertently fall into your lap, you need to be a student of your organizational chart. There's nothing worse for customers, for example, than calling an 800 number with a frustrating problem, being placed on hold, and when finally connected to a live body discovering the service representative can't help them—and has little clue about who else in the company to send them to for assistance.

Know who the "go to" people are in your organization. Take time to learn the various responsibilities and skill sets of people in departments you may one day have to call upon for help—or transfer lost customers to. Remember that knocking customers' socks off is almost always a team effort.

Creating a seamless service experience for customers also depends on understanding your own place in the "cycle of service." In other words, do you know who in your organization depends on you to do a timely and competent job? Do you know what happens to your work once it leaves your computer screen, cubicle, or department? At Dun & Bradstreet, the giant data management and research company, every employee is required to answer two questions to identify their key internal partners, no matter where on the organizational ladder they may be: *Who does my work go to? Who is my work important to?*

If you're taking customer orders in a call center, for example, where do those orders go? What happens if essential information is missing from those orders or entered incorrectly? Your internal partners in warehouse, billing, or shipping will be the ones who have to deal with irate customers when orders aren't received on time, names are spelled incorrectly, or packages sent to the wrong address.

Delighting customers often depends on the ability of employees from different departments to put aside differences and work hand-in-glove to meet quality or service goals. In the airline business, maintenance workers make it possible for ground crews and pilots to keep planes flying on time, and catering staff keeps the planes well-stocked with food and beverages so flight attendants can keep passengers fed and comfortable. If there is a breakdown in those service delivery systems—if someone misses a deadline or passes shoddy work downstream to others—it's external customers who pay the price.

> **TIP:** Once you've identified your key internal partners, talk to them about what they do and don't like about the service you provide for them. Use their feedback to improve the quality of work you do.

Toward One-stop Service

There will be times when you have to "call in the cavalry" to solve difficult customer problems or requests, situations when you'll have to transfer callers to experts in your company or get back to them after doing more research. But your chief goal should be to address customer issues in "one stop." Nothing pleases customers like having their questions answered or problems resolved with one easy, hassle-free contact with your company.

The customer service research firm TARP in Arlington, Virginia, found one of the most important factors for customers in deciding whether to keep their business with a company was "providing a satisfactory response to questions or issues on first contact." Customers don't like to have to call back a second or third time to resolve their issues, nor are they thrilled by being bounced to additional contact points in an organization when seeking answers.

Be relentless in your efforts to satisfy customer requests in "one stop." Strive to be like the service representatives at QVC, the world's top televised shopping service, who are taught to transfer calls only as a last resort. The mantra at QVC is "one call, one person" and service reps are given the training and support to make it happen. "The last thing we want is for customers to have to call our centers back about the same issue," says John Hunter, a QVC customer service executive. "Our goal is 100 percent first-call resolution."

Avoiding "It's Not My Job" Syndrome

Providing seamless service also is about taking the initiative to help customers even when that duty seems to fall outside the boundaries of your normal job. We know of one customer service agent for Delta Airlines, for example, who was on duty one day at the Cincinnati airport when she came upon a woman who had taken ill. The woman, who had two children and spoke little English, needed to go to a hospital immediately. While some service agents would have simply pointed her to the airport taxi area or pleaded ignorance of the foreign

language, this Delta agent instead accompanied the woman and her children to the hospital. When the sick woman was released, the agent took the travelers home and put them up for the night, and the next day she drove them back to the airport and got them boarded for home.

While you can't be expected to perform this kind of "above and beyond" service every day, the example provides a lesson about lending a hand when others are in need. Think about how you've felt in the past, for example, when you've taken a problem to a service provider and had them respond with, "Wish I could help, but that's not my job" and then had them do little or nothing to find others to help you in the organization.

Nothing says Knock Your Socks Off Service to customers or co-workers like a willingness to go out of your way and do just that little extra to help meet their needs.

> "We got to get back to a fundamental issue, and that is: We all work first for the customer."
>
> —Louis V Gerstner, Jr.,
> former CEO, IBM Corp.

21

Exceptional Service Is in the Details

"It is just the little touches after the average man would quit that make the master's fame."

—Orison Swett Marden
Founder, *Success* magazine

Asked about the difference between memorable and mundane buildings, German architect Mies van der Rohe responded simply, "God is in the details, the details, the details." What's true of quality architecture is true of quality service: If you pay attention to the details, the right details, customers will notice and come back for more. That attention to detail communicates to customers that tangibles are important to you and your organization.

Everything Counts

The details surround us, no matter what kind of job we do. It's how we look, and how our workplace looks, how our web page looks and how much bandwidth it has. It's how we speak and what we say. It's all the little extra courtesies and comforts we build into the service experience—or the myriad nagging annoyances we lose track of and make our customers wade through to do business with us.

Attention to details is a prime characteristic of high-performing organizations. The cast members at Disney World have a passion for details that make customers sit up and take notice. A colleague of ours raves about Shirley, the house-keeper she met during a recent vacation to Disney World. "The first day, when we checked in, I saw the 'Your room was cleaned by Shirley. Have a great stay' note. I noticed the 'I' in Shirley was dotted with a little Mickey. That was cute, but we were at Disney. The third day Shirley really wowed me. I'd left a note asking for more towels. When we returned to the room, there was a "Do not disturb" sign on our bathroom door. Inside, Shirley had taken our morning paper and the eye-glasses I'd left by the sink, and arranged the extra towels in the form of a man sitting on the toilet reading the daily paper. "I laughed so loud. I don't think I'll ever forget that!"

A growing number of managers and executives today understand that the examples they model in turn set a positive tone for their organizations. For example:

- Fred Smith, the founder and chairman of FedEx, begins many of his visits to FedEx facilities in far-flung cities by hopping on a delivery van and going out on the road with a FedEx courier.
- Bill Marriott, Jr., chairman and CEO of Marriott International, often takes a turn at the hotel registration desk checking in guests; he also empties ashtrays in the lobby and picks up trash in the parking lot.
- And there isn't a manager at Walt Disney World or Disneyland who doesn't personally pick up, straighten, and worry after the thousand and one details that create an unparalleled experience for their customers.

These executives model attention to detail for their employees, just as you model it for customers and co-workers.

The Moments of Truth

Attention to detail is more than playing at or being a janitor. It is the way you remember—and remind others—that contact with any aspect of your work group gives your customers an opportunity to form positive or negative impressions. We refer to these opportunities as Moments of Truth.

A Moment of Truth occurs anytime a customer comes in contact with any part of your organization and uses that contact to judge the quality of the organization.

Anything and everything can become a Moment of Truth for your customers: the look of your store, building, or parking lot; the promises made in your advertising; how long your phone rings before being answered, and how the call is handled; how sensitively you respond to a problem they're having; how long it takes before an e-mail is responded to; how customer concerns are addressed in social media or chat rooms, . . . plus the memorable personal contacts your customers have with you.

Managing the Moments of Truth

When you began your current job, your orientation and training probably focused on the primary Moments of Truth built into your position. If you have been with your company for a long time, you've probably learned to recognize many more Moments of Truth that are important to your customers. To deliver true Knock Your Socks Off Service, you have to manage each and every Moment of Truth individually.

> **TIP:** The way that Moments of Truth are managed determines the grades customers give you on their mental report cards. Manage the moments well, and you receive A's and B's—and earn a repeat customer. Manage them poorly, and you earn D's and F's—and lose a customer in the bargain. Work to get good grades in this particular school and you'll find your diploma has cash value.

Over time, it's easy to think you've mastered all the various moments of truth your customers might present you with. Don't believe it! No matter how experienced and skillful you become, you can always count on your customers to come up with something new. That's because customers can turn almost anything into a Moment of Truth.

To truly master the Moments of Truth in your services, develop these three customer-focused habits:

1. *Never stop learning.* The details that are important to your customers change from day to day as well as from customer to customer. At one time it might be speed of response they're concerned with; at another ensuring the information you provide them with is exhaustively researched, thorough, and accurate; at another it might be what technological methods are available for doing business with you. There's always more to know.
2. *Ask your customers.* The only reliable way to identify your customers' particular, peculiar Moments of Truth is to get them to describe those moments to you.
3. *Ask your company.* In addition to your own informal, day-to-day observations of customer preferences, your company probably conducts continuing surveys and studies. Make sure you know what the researchers know that will help you serve your customers better.

Remember, it's not the tigers and bears that chase the customers away. What bugs the customer the most are the mosquitoes and the gnats—the little things.

> "Commit yourself to performing one ten-minute act of exceptional customer service per day and to inducing your colleagues to do the same. In a 100–person outfit, taking into account normal vacations, holidays, etc., that would mean 24,000 new courteous acts per year. Such is the stuff of revolutions."
>
> —Tom Peters

22

Good Selling Is Good Service—Good Service Is Good Selling

"Nothing happens until someone sells something."

—Marketing axiom

Sales and service are not separate functions. They are two sides of the same coin. Even if your title is customer service representative and a co-worker is a sales associate, you both have the same ultimate goal: satisfying the customer. It wasn't always this way. In days gone by, sales and service personnel used to be adversaries.

Sales and marketing people viewed their counterparts in service and operations as "those guys who never want to help me make a sale and who screw it up after it's a done deal."

Service and operations folk, for their part, tended to view sales and marketing people as "those people in suits who write outlandish ads, make ridiculous promises to close a sale, and leave us holding the bag with the customer."

In today's world, sales, marketing, service, and operations share a common goal: creating and retaining customers.

When Lines Overlap

To create and retain customers, we have to combine good selling with good service. Consider the case of Edgar Pinchpenny III, the unhappy owner of a Model 412-A Handy-Andy Cordless Electric Screwdriver. (You know he's unhappy because he is waving the 412-A around, banging it on the desk and demanding his money back.)

Using your very best Knock Your Socks Off Service skills (listening—questioning—problem solving), you determine that Pinchpenny is upset because the 412-A needs frequent recharging and isn't very powerful. But you also know that the 412-A was built for small repair jobs around the house. It absolutely was not designed for the industrial strength, barn-building, automobile overhaul sort of work Pinchpenny is trying to get out of it. That's why your company also sells the much more expensive 412-C Turbo-Andy, the best professional power screwdriver in the industry and the perfect tool for Pinchpenny's job.

Better service at the time of the original sale _might_ have matched Pinchpenny with the more appropriate tool. But what should you do about the situation now? Tighten the chin strap on your thinking cap and consider which of these four possible actions you would recommend:

Option 1: Tell Pinchpenny that if he hadn't been too cheap to buy the proper tools in the first place, he wouldn't be standing here screaming himself into a coronary.

Option 2: Explain the limitations of the 412-A and the benefits of the 412-C to Pinchpenny, and recommend that he consider buying _up_.

Option 3: Apologize to Pinchpenny for the inconvenience, explain the difference between the two models, offer to personally make an exchange on the spot, and give him a discount on the 412-C to compensate for being inconvenienced.

Option 4: Apologize for the salesperson's incompetence, offer Pinchpenny an even exchange—the old, abused

412-A for a shiny new 412-C at no additional cost—
throw in a free set of your best stainless steel screwdriver bits *and* offer to wash Pinchpenny's car.

We pick Option 3 as the best course of action: It shows
concern, responsiveness, and good salesmanship. It doesn't
unduly punish Pinchpenny for the human error involved in
the original purchase—whether his or yours. Nor does it unduly reward him for his argumentative, and unpleasant,
return behavior. Option 2 is a narrow, old-fashioned, service-
as-complaint-department response. It isn't likely to keep
Pinchpenny as a long-term customer. Options 1 and 4 are the
kind of answers suitable for companies where frontline people
are specifically recruited with IQs approximately equal to
their shoe sizes.

When Selling Is Not Good Service

There are three situations in which selling is not good service:

1. *When there are no alternatives.* The customer's needs
   cannot be met by any product or service you offer, regardless of how well you can fix the problem, answer
   the question, or explain the current product or service.
2. *When there is no slack.* You know how to solve the
   problem, but the customer came to you mad, has
   stayed mad, and obviously wants to stay mad. There is
   very little chance to make the customer unmad, let
   alone sell an upgrade or a switch to a different model.
3. *When there is no point.* An upgrade or add-on would be
   totally illogical, unrelated, or inappropriate to the situation, as in, "Would you like some garlic bread to go with
   your cappuccino this morning?" or "Ma'am, this new
   plan could save you up to $60 on your new telephone
   bill" when the customer's entire bill is just $35 per
   month. Make sure you're offering customers something
   that is relevant and appropriate to their situation.

When Selling Is Good Service

There are five situations in which selling is good service:

1. *When the product or service the customer is using is wrong*—but you know which model, system, or approach will better fit the customer's needs and are in a position to get it for the customer. "It's going to be difficult to get the fast downloads you want on podcast or photo files with your current dial-up service. You might want to consider upgrading to our new digital service to get the speed and performance you're after."

2. *When the product or service the customer acquired from your company is right*—but some other part, program, or process is needed before your product or service will perform properly: "Your computer operating system is Windows 2003. Our software is designed for Windows 7. I do know of an upgrade for Windows 2003 that might work."

3. *When the product or service in question is out of date*—"I can send you a new widget and walk you through the repair when you receive it. I also think it would be a good idea to consider a newer model that will do the job better. The Laser XJ7 has improved circuitry and can . . ."

4. *When an add-on feature will forestall other problems*—"I see you decided against extended warranty protection. Since you've had two problems during the warranty period, I wonder if you shouldn't reconsider that decision?"

5. *When changing the customer to a different product or service will be seen as value-added or TLC*—"This checking account requires a very high minimum balance. That's what caused the service charge you are concerned about. I'd like to recommend a different plan that I think will fit your needs better and save you from incurring future charges."

If it says customer service on your name tag, then serving the customer is your full-time occupation. But remember: Even if nothing in your job description hints at a sales responsibility, you are a part of the sales and marketing team. Yours is always a two-hat job.

"In reality, selling and service are inseparable."
>   —Leonard Berry, David Bennett, Carter Brown
>   *Service Quality*

23

Communicating with Customers in the Digital Age

"The more high tech the world becomes, the more people crave high-touch service."

—John Naisbett, Megatrends

Face-to-face, phone call, e-mail, online chat, text, blogging, Twitter, social media, digital video—that's just the start of a list of communication mediums. The options that today's customer has to communicate with an organization are seemingly growing by the week.

What does that mean for you, the customer service professional? It means you have to be on top of your game like never before! It's no longer enough to just have the right pace and tone on the phone with customers, you've got to expand your repertoire and become a service master in all these communication mediums.

Let's take a look at some of the most popular.

E-Mail and Telephone

There's no question that e-mail has essentially become the communication tool of choice these days. However, sometimes it's more valuable and effective, not to mention efficient, to make a quick phone call to get the information you need. A call has the added value of enabling you to establish a connection and build a relationship with your customer.

Andrew Pearce, chief executive of Powwownow, offers this quick summary of when it's best to use e-mail and when a phone call might be a better choice. (We'll learn more about the do's and don'ts of e-mails in the following chapter.)

When e-mail is a good choice:

- *Keep a record of the communication.* In instances when it will be beneficial to have a digital record of a specific conversation, delivery of a document, or verbal agreement to a price or a project, e-mail is a very effective tool.
- *Keep track of details.* You know the old saying, "the devil is in the details." It's an apt description for those pesky but often critically important parts of a transaction, project, plan, or contract. By capturing those details in an e-mail, you reduce the risk of overlooking something important and you create a record for others to reference.
- *Follow-up.* This is probably the second best use of e-mail, especially after meeting or speaking with a new prospect or customer. This simple step allows you to continue the dialogue with your customer and communicate your enthusiasm or organizational capabilities, or to say thank you.
- *Provide status updates and customer feedback.* E-mail makes it very simple to provide brief status updates, easily keeping customers in the loop, or to summarize patterns or trends in customer feedback for supervisors and colleagues.

Of course, e-mail often tends to venture into those sensitive subjects better left to a phone call. In fact, e-mail has become a convenient replacement for difficult discussions. Why suffer through the anxiety of an uncomfortable conversation when you can send a chipper e-mail and hopefully avoid it altogether? That's a brilliant plan, but it does your customer a disservice. It's in these and countless other situations when a phone call is the better option.

When the phone is a good choice:

- *Sensitive Subjects or Details*. Often a personal touch and the ability to respond immediately to a complaint or concern is the best way to solve the problem. Personally informing your customers of a problem as soon as you become aware of it wins extra points in the RATER assessment. Customers may not be happy, but they will appreciate being kept informed.
- *E-Mail Overload*. When too much e-mail or too many details start flowing, it's easy to lose track of a conversation. Sometimes a brief phone conversation is needed to cut through the in-box clutter.
- *Tone*. Sometimes you need to hear what the other person isn't saying. Most of us have learned the hard way that sarcasm doesn't always translate well via e-mail. There are times when it's important to hear the voice inflections, pauses, or even silence that a phone call can reveal.
- *First Impression*. When you're introducing yourself, your company, or your proposal and face-to-face interaction isn't possible, a phone call is the next best way to make a good first impression. No matter how well written or engaging your e-mail content, it simply cannot deliver the same experience.
- *Clarity*. When you need to review details or actions outlined in writing, the phone is a better choice. A few minutes by phone to walk through a document or plan allows both your customer and you to provide additional detail or clarity on the subject.

As Knock Your Socks Off Service providers, we need to become adept at various kinds of communication with our customers. True, e-mail allows more flexibility and allows us to "shoot out an e-mail and cross it off our list." But take care to remember the needs of your customer. Has your customer had a negative experience with you? A warm phone call to follow up and see how she's doing or if you can offer any additional assistance can work wonders in restoring the company back into the customer's good graces. Never forget the impact of a personal touch.

Online Chat

You're navigating a web page checking out various products, everything is going swimmingly, when suddenly you realize that you can't figure out which of the models you're looking at includes headphones, and which does not. Out of the corner of your eye you see a small pop up screen appear, "My name is Tanya, May I help you?"

Eagerly you click on Tanya's warm greeting and your computer temporarily freezes while you wait and wait and wait for Tanya to finally connect with you. Finally, Tanya appears in a chat box, reintroduces herself, asks for your name, and then asks how she might help you.

Quickly you type in the two model numbers you're considering, and your request to know which one includes headphones.

Tanya responds quickly, "We typically list all features included with each item in the item description. Does this answer your question?"

After letting out a frustrated sigh, you try again, "No, not quite. Yes, I realize that information is usually listed; however, I'm unable to see it on this particular model."

You tense up waiting for Tanya's reply and you imagine her sighing in frustration as well, "I see. Let me do some quick checking and see what I can find out for you. . .thank you for your patience."

You check a couple of e-mails while you await Tanya's return, all the while wondering if perhaps you've been disconnected, no. . . . it appears she's still there. Finally, after a "long" wait of probably 3 minutes, Tanya replies, "Jill, I've done some checking and both models include the headphones. The first one you listed offers an ear bud, and the other is the original headphone styling. Is there anything else I may assist you with today?"

Hot dog! You got the answer you needed! You didn't have to wait in a long phone queue, you didn't have to wait for someone to respond to your e-mail, and you didn't have to risk ordering the wrong item! Tanya had indeed saved the day! You quickly respond, "No, Tanya, thanks so much for your help—that's all I need!"

Seconds later Tanya responds with, "Have a nice day and thank you for shopping with us." And clicks off!

What could be easier, simpler, and more productive! Many companies are leaving their customers frustrated by not offering this service. True, it's not for all organizations, but think about it—is this a way you could better serve your customers?

Online Chat Etiquette

It's easy to think that Tanya just knew what to do in order to make Jill's day brighter. But here are a few online chat tips that might be beneficial:

1. Convey warmth by stating the customer's name a few times during the chat.
2. Remember to pay close attention to customer questions—asking a customer to repeat herself conveys that you're not paying attention.
3. Frame responses in a positive light, rather than saying "I have absolutely no idea what you're talking about," say something like "That's a good question, let me find out for you. Are you able to hold for a moment?"
4. Don't be afraid to script some warm, friendly responses—but don't rely on them exclusively.
5. Use good grammar and communication skills.
6. Proof your response *before* hitting the send button.

A Word about Texting

Without question, texting has taken the world by storm over the past few years. Kids won't answer phone calls from parents, but will send an immediate reply in response to a text. It's tempting to bring this fast, efficient tool into the work-place. However, here are a few things to keep in mind:

1. Texting is extremely informal. It can be very difficult to create a professional, well thought out message in 160 characters or less.
2. Texting can also be difficult to track. Often, texts are set to automatically erase after being sent—that means once a message is read it's easily gone, never to be seen again. That can prove difficult if something is misread or misunderstood.
3. Texting can be seen as not only informal, but also too personal for the workplace. Your customers may not appreciate having you text them on their personal phones in the middle of their work day. It may be inappropriate.
4. Texting will never replace the professionalism of a phone call. Don't treat your relationship with your customer too lightly. If your customer feels you're not taking him or his business seriously, he might consider the competition.
5. There is definitely a time and a place for texting. Think, double think, and triple think before sending "TY. . .ttyl" as a way of communicating with your customer.

Corporate Web Sites

Corporate web sites offer a great place to build communities. Community simply means that a site is more than a place to buy; it's a place to learn, share, and communicate with others. It allows visitors to make the site their own by joining a conversation or learning new facts. Adding community is actually a fairly cheap addition to any web site because visitors create the bulk of the content. Another huge payoff is that the organization—you—are more in control. You have the ability to address problems, questions, or misinformation quickly and cleanly.

As a Knock Your Socks Off Service professional, the interaction you have with your customer is a great place to test out this concept. Ask you customer what more your organization can offer them in terms of product information, applications, or service deals. As a listening post for your company, this contribution is valuable for all. And remember: the fewer human contacts people have with your organization, the more important each one becomes.

The World of Social Media

Social media is everywhere! It's used for businesses and keeping in touch with friends, and it is a great way for your customers to leave feedback on their experience with your organization. Consumers now have a quick outlet to vent their frustrations to any encounter—and it's no longer limited to just your web site's feedback portal. They have numerous avenues at their disposal: Facebook, Yelp, CityBiz, Blogs, YouTube, Twitter, MySpace, Diggit, and more.

Bottom line? Customers who reach out to you via digital mediums are no different than those that communicate via the old stand-by forms of communication. They want to be listened to, responded to, and be treated with dignity and respect.

"Technology doesn't try harder, people do."

—Avis Advertisement

24

Putting Your Best E-Mail Foot Forward

"When you introduce yourself via e-mail, not only are you making a first impression, you're also leaving a written record."

—Virginia Shea, Netiquette™ Guru

Today many organizations regularly communicate with their customers via e-mail. Sometimes that e-mail comes through the company's commercial web site, other times it comes through an ISP (Internet service provider) like AOL, MSN, Yahoo, or Google.

Regardless of the route e-mail follows to get to your screen, there are both customer expectations and protocols to observe when you are providing customer service by e-mail. Customers judge online service by how easy a company is to contact and how quickly and accurately questions are answered. And while your organization may have a fabulously robust frequently asked questions (FAQ) section on its web site, customer opinion of "e-service" will more likely rest on the quality and speed of your response to their e-mail questions and complaints than on a static self-service feature.

Remember, to your customers you are the company—even in the disembodied age of the Internet. Your organization can send out thousands of e-mails each day, but all it takes is one poorly worded, offensive, or robotic response to ruin its reputation.

The E-Mail Customer

Just as the over-the-phone customer doesn't think much of you if their call isn't answered in one or two rings, the e-mail customer isn't impressed if it takes two or three days to receive a reply to a question or complaint. Think of it this way: If someone put you on hold for two days, how happy would that make you? Customers expect e-mail to be almost as fast as the telephone. After all, they reason, the whole thing works by computer, shouldn't it be fast? Add the use of Twitter and the pace of communication increases exponentially. Many organizations now have service teams monitoring the chatter to respond instantly. If your customer has ever had that type of interaction, the expectation is that an e-mail response will be nearly immediate.

> **TIP:** The standard reply time expectation for business e-mails is about 8 hours, but headed down— fast. In some industries, two to four hours is now considered the norm. If you can't make a same-day reply to a customer inquiry, you should at least acknowledge receipt of the message the same day. Some web sites do this automatically. If yours doesn't, acknowledge the message and tell the sender when you will have a reply.

Replying to E-Mails

Many people are used to "conversing" in a chatty, informal way with their friends over the Internet. The speed and perceived informality of e-mail make the medium feel more conversational than writing a letter. But be careful! Do not treat customers like old friends—unless they are. And take care in the language you use with customers. Unless you are writing to someone who is very familiar with your business, avoid jargon and shorthand expressions; your customer may not know what a POS display or XD29 system is. It's also dangerous to assume that anyone who sends you electronic mail is familiar with all of the uniqueness and conventions of e-mail. For example, people who use e-mail frequently often use acronyms, such as IMHO (in my humble opinion) and BTW (by the way), and put emoticons, symbols that convey emotions, in their correspondence.

When writing e-mail, think about the characteristics of the person who's on the receiving end of your message:

- Is your reader young or old? A high-level executive or a newly hired college graduate? Is English his or her first language? Make sure your customers will understand what you write and be comfortable with the way you write it. Even with young, Internet-savvy customers, loose language and flip remarks can be misunderstood. And older customers can be more offended than other generational groups by a lack of formality or deference in your messages.
- What's the nature of your relationship with this customer? If you haven't corresponded with this person much before, err on the side of being more formal and

deferential. If the customer is upset with something don't try "kidding" or cajoling them regardless of how well you know them.

- Get to the point. Don't make readers slog through 30 lines of text before they get to the real point of your message. Avoid excessive "throat clearing" by stating the purpose of the e-mail soon after your opening greeting.

- Reread your correspondence again carefully before you push "send." Look at the tone. A cold, impersonal tone, for instance, tells customers you're thinking of them like a number. Too much jargon and legalese will confuse rather than comfort, and make them wonder if you have something to hide. And spelling counts in e-mail as well. If you didn't care enough to spell check, what does that tell the customer about how you'll handle the rest of his needs?

- Make sure the right people receive your message. Too often e-mailers automatically hit the reply button and send or "cc" a message to many who don't need to see it, or to whom the message is a low-priority or even irrelevant issue. In some cases, what are intended as confidential messages are sent to those who shouldn't see them. Ditto for blindly forwarding messages that you receive to customers or co-workers. It's tedious to have to scroll through a long list of others' e-mail addresses before you get to the "needle in the haystack"— the message itself. Always check your "reply to" list carefully before you hit send.

TIP: Be careful when sending e-mail attachments to customers. For starters, make sure the person you're sending the attachment to has the right software to be able to read it. Some companies also have policies against receiving attachments to avoid viruses that might be contained in them or to limit the downloading of large files that can stress their private networks. When in doubt, check with customers to make sure it's OK to send an attachment before doing so.

The Outcome

Think about the action you want to encourage. It should be clear from what you've written why you are writing and what, if anything, you expect your customers to do in response. Do they need to take any action? If so, by what date and in what form? Are they supposed to retain the correspondence for future reference? If so, for how long? Do they need to pass it along to someone else? If so, to whom and by when? Good writing is an extremely powerful part of good service. Inept writing undermines everything you've worked so hard to build.

THREE E-MAIL TIPS*

1. Be personal. While e-mail to customers should be more formal than e-mail to friends or co-workers, e-mail users have come to expect electronic communication to have a more personal style. Nothing leaves customers as cold as a canned response to a problem or concern that's been keeping them up at night. Whenever possible, personalize your e-mail by using your own name, customizing responses to a customer's questions, and including a thoughtful sign-off.
2. Think like a 1950s Smith Corona typewriter. With so many people sending and receiving e-mail from Blackberrys, iPhones, Droids, and other 3G devices, it's very common to receive e-mail that doesn't include special characters, bullets, bold, underlining, or tabs. Take care that your e-mail is simple, clear, and easy to read.
3. Don't YELL. Using all capital letters to communicate is the e-mail equivalent of constant bellowing. While caps may be used for emphasis, consider other methods, such as surrounding text with *asterisks* to indicate italics, or __underscores__ to indicate underlining.

* These three tips have been adapted from *Netiquette* (TM) by Virginia Shea (Albion Books, 1994).

Personalization

When you are responding to e-mail queries, personalized messages hold much more value than computer-generated responses in the customer's eyes. The personal response tells the customer that you are interested in helping them do business with you. If your company has an Internet shopping site, personalization is the most obvious, straightforward way to uplift the shopper's experience. A joint study by the Society of Consumer Affairs Professionals (SOCAP) and Yankelovich Partners found that only one percent of online shoppers surveyed felt an automated response—a generic reply—to their problem situations was acceptable. Customers base their opinion of your company on the way their inquiries and problems are responded to. Consider the following real-life customer e-mails and the customer service representative (CSR) responses and think of where they could serve as models for making your own customer correspondence more personal.

From a customer:

Hello,

I'm considering ordering a holiday Fab Five Cookie wreath—even though it's after Christmas. Will it last until next Christmas, or will it decay? I couldn't tell if it was a real or permanent wreath.

The reply:

Dear Disney Guest

Thank you for your e-mail.

Below is the information you requested regarding item #20228, the Fab Five Cookie Wreath.

Because the wreath has sugar cookies on it, the cookies will probably not be good by next Christmas. The actual wreath is a faux wreath and is not real, so you can enjoy that for many years to come.

If we can be of any further assistance, please let us know.

Sincerely,
DisneyStore.com

From a customer:

Hello,

I'm considering purchasing a 7-wood golf club—can you tell me how this will improve my game?

Dave

The reply:

Dave,

A seven-wood takes the place of your three iron. You can also use it out of the rough, if the ball is sitting high, but normally it will take the place of the three iron. On long tough shots where the ball will be hard to get up in the air, it will take its place. It is good off the tee and long iron shots!

Hit'em long and straight!
Have a great day!

Andrew Reichert
Fogdog.com
The Ultimate Sports Store

"She's thrilled to be answering 95% of customers' e-mails within 3 days. (Doesn't she know that within hours most went straight to her competitor's sites?)"

—Genesys advertisement

25

Responding Positively to Negative Feedback

"We'd better take care of our customers, or someone else will."

—Gary Richard, President and CEO, P.C.
Richard and Son, Inc.

It wasn't long ago that responding to customer feedback was a straightforward exercise. Customers would phone a call center, fire off an e-mail, or offer in-person feedback when they sought to contact you with a problem or weigh in on the quality of your products or services. That, of course, is a bygone era. With the proliferation of social networks, customer review sites, and the growing number of discussion boards used by companies on their own web sites, millions of customer opinions are floating around cyberspace at any given moment. Monitoring what's being said about you online, then taking time to respond where appropriate, is critical in today's business environment.

To Engage or Not Engage

Once you've identified what's being said about you and where most of that discussion is occurring, you face a weighty deci-

sion: whether to react to the customer commentary. Not all negative feedback is created equal. Here are some guidelines for
when you should respond to customer comments or reviews:

• *When you've obviously erred.* Sometimes your company
has clearly messed up. This means apologizing for the error,
offering to fix the problem, and in some cases providing atonement for the breakdown. It also means making a promise to
improve next time around.
• *When a negative review shows signs of going viral.* It's
tempting to sit back and do nothing if you think a negative review or opinion is wildly off base. What may appear to be isolated cases of service problems tucked away in the far corners
of the Internet can quickly blow up and spread like wildfire. If
you're seeing a trend of negative comments, that's a signal to
take a deep breath, investigate, and try to contain the damage.
• *If customers are misrepresenting your products or services.* Customers sometimes get it wrong! When a warranty is
misstated or your prices are misquoted, or they're bashing the
buffalo burger they ordered at your restaurant when there is
no such item on your menu—you'll want to gracefully step in
and clarify the facts.
• *When the reviews are positive.* You might think there's
little need to follow up on positive reviews, but responding
can have multiple benefits. Your goal should be only to
deliver a simple thank-you and let the reviewer know you
appreciate the time they took to comment. That can only
increase the odds that they'll stay loyal to you in the future.

As a Knock Your Socks Off Service professional, be sure
you know the boundaries and authority you have to make the
decision to respond and how best to do that.

All Eyes on You

Every day you engage untold numbers of customers. Although
the outcome of these individual interactions might not decide
your organization's fate, taken as a whole they determine
whether your company is perceived as one that values and

respects customers or one that views them as a necessary nuisance. Each customer touch-point, whether conducting a mundane transaction or handling a potentially catastrophic problem, is a Moment of Truth that should be approached with the same forethought and care. How you respond to customer questions, problems, product reviews, rants, or kudos is the litmus test of service quality. That's because to the customer, you are the company!

Responding to customers in a calm, professional, and service-sensitive way is an art form that takes on even greater importance in public venues. It takes training in how to respond appropriately to multiple scenarios. Whether via written word, phone, or face-to-face interaction, all the best empathy, listening, questioning, and problem-solving skills still apply.

Responding to Negative Feedback

Regardless of the form of the feedback—in person, on the phone, via e-mail, on Twitter, or through a review site—there are important things to remember:

• *People want to engage with people.* Be conversational in your response and talk like a normal person. This isn't the time to use multisyllabic words, corporatespeak, language sanitized by attorneys, or industry acronyms. The human contact makes the customer feel valued and important, and it allows them to tell their story. It allows for genuine exchange.

• *Work to respond promptly.* Speediness sends a sign to customers that you care, that feedback is important to your organization. And that you're not afraid to work to help a customer and make it better.

• *Avoid excuses or trying to spin the situation to make yourself look like a victim.* The idea is to be open, honest, and sincere. If you know you contributed to a problem in some way or if some part of your company is in obvious need of improvement, apologize sincerely, work to defuse the situation, and describe what you'll change to ensure that the customer doesn't experience the same problem again.

• *Above all, never, ever lose your head.* The moment you go ballistic or start hurling insults, you've lost the battle. When possible, take at least 30 minutes after receiving negative feedback to respond to the customer. Remember to stay calm, focus on the customer and listen, listen, listen. The customer is likely to have some truth in what she is saying.

Take It Offline

Eric Groves, Sr. Vice President Global Market Development for Constant Contact, posted an interesting blog (August 2010) about public vs. private responses. It garnered many a comment. He says:

> "Every business loves social media marketing when customers are raving about them in Facebook status updates and tweets, but what happens when there's some bad press on a social network? How do you handle a potential public blemish without making it into a full-fledged stain? While the downside of social media marketing is that we cannot control what people say about our businesses, we can use these powerful connectors to make things right."

Eric proceeds to suggest that the best strategy is to take the public rant to a private connection—or offline. Once you have the customer in personal contact, it's easier to do the Knock Your Socks Off work you know how to do—apologize, empathize, listen, learn, fix the person, fix the problem, and be quick about it!

Another perspective is that customers recognize that companies aren't perfect. One responder to this blog (Doogie) made valid these points:

> "How you respond in public says a LOT about your brand for everyone to see. There's value in that. If I can see that you handle complaints and negative publicity with grace, charm, wit, and a sincere desire

to resolve the issue, then as an onlooker, I've just gotten a really positive view of your business.

You've let me see that I'm going to be a happy customer if I deal with you.

You also give me the opportunity to become an evangelist by seeing that you've done everything you can for the customer.

If someone brings a problem to you publicly one should *always* respond publicly—even if to tell that person "I will contact you privately."

My advice—don't be afraid of negative publicity or complaints. Embrace them as an opportunity to satisfy that customer and impress onlookers with the quality of your customer service."

As you can see, there is a balancing act to be performed when making decisions about public vs. private contact. The decision to go offline might depend on the length of the discussion. If you can resolve the issue quickly, do it in public. If it looks like the disagreement is degrading into a knockdown, drag-out fight, take it offline. How well you respond to customer questions, reviews, problems, and suggestions—and whether you get that response right the first time—separates the customer service champs from the pretenders.

> "Total quality customer service cannot be stored in inventory; it must be 100% available on demand."
>
> —Unknown

26

Never Underestimate the Value of a Sincere Thank-You

"Thank You . . . thank you, thank you . . . and thank you!!!"

—Fozzie Bear

Remember when you were ten years old and what you wanted for your birthday was that electric train or special Barbie? And your grandmother gave you underwear instead. And your mom and dad stood there and looked at you and pinched you on the arm. "Now, what do you say?" they prompted. "Thank you, Grandma," you said. And your grandma beamed and patted you on the head.

Saying "thank you" is as important today as it was when your parents tried so hard to drum it into your head. In your job, you need to say "thanks" to your customers every day. You need to sincerely value the gift of business they bring you—even if it may not be as exciting as electric trains and Barbie dolls.

Nine Times When You Should Thank Customers

1. *When they do business with you . . . every time.* It bears repeating: Customers have options every time they

139

need a service or product. There are few barriers keeping them from shifting their business to your organization's competitors. It's easy to take regular and walk-in customers for granted. It's even easier to forget to thank a one-time Internet customer—out of (web) site, out of mind. Don't make that costly mistake. Thank them for choosing to do business with you.

2. *When they compliment you (or your company).* Compliments can be embarrassing. But shrugging off customers' sincere praise says, "You dummy, I'm not really that good." Instead, accept it gracefully. Say, "Thank you," and add, "I really appreciate your business and learning what we are doing right."

3. *When they offer comments or suggestions.* Thanking customers for feedback says that you've heard what they had to say and value their opinion. Saying something as simple as "Thank you for taking the time to tell me that. It really helps us know where we can do better," can work wonders.

4. *When they try a new product or service.* Trying something new can be uncomfortable. And risky. After all, the old and familiar is so, well, old and familiar. Thank customers for daring to try something different.

5. *When they recommend you to a friend.* When customers recommend you they put themselves on the line. If you deliver, they look good. If you don't. . . . A written thank you for a recommendation or a value-added token the next time you encounter these customers says you value their referrals.

6. *When they are patient . . . and not so patient.* Whether they tell you about it or not (and, boy, will some customers tell you about it!), no one likes to wait. Thanking customers for their patience says you noticed and value their time. It's also one of the quickest ways to defuse customers who have waited too long and are none too happy about it.

7. *When they help you to serve them better.* Some customers are always prepared. They have their account

numbers right at their fingertips, always bring the right forms, and keep notes on their previous service calls. They make your life a lot easier—make a point of thanking them for it.

8. *When they complain to you.* Thank them for complaining? Absolutely! Customers who tell you they are unhappy are giving you a second chance. And that's quite a gift. Now you have a chance to win their renewed loyalty, which will give you additional opportunities to thank them in the future.

9. *When they make you smile.* A smile is one of the greatest gifts you can receive. Saying thank you just makes it better.

Three Ways to Say Thank You

1. *Verbally.* Say it after every encounter. And say it with feeling. The phrase "thank-you-for-shopping-at-our-store. . . next?" said like a freight train roaring past does little to impress customers. Make your thank-yous warm, pleasant, and personal.

2. *In writing.* Send a follow-up e-mail after a purchase or visit. Personalize it. Customers hate form letters. Write a thank you at the bottom of invoices or bills. Or go out of your way and send a personal note via snail mail. Your customers will be shocked and will appreciate the gesture much more than a quick e-mail—but do both! Customers want the immediate thank you that the e-mail provides—the handwritten note . . . icing on the cake!!

3. *With a gift.* Give something small, like a notepad or pen imprinted with your company name. It will help customers remember your business. For the right customer, an enjoyable e-mail graphic is a good thank-you card—but be very careful and selective; tastes differ widely. (And beware, the computer firewalls in some companies might delete your greeting before they get to the intended recipient.)

TIP: Make sure the value of the gift isn't out of balance with the nature of the business involved. Some customers worry that more expensive gifts may be an attempt to buy their business, rather than a token of appreciation. Additionally, it's generally considered inappropriate to send a tangible gift to a government client under any circumstances.

Five Often-Forgotten Thank-Yous

1. *Thank your co-workers.* Give credit to those who help you. We all have those special, go-to people that we know are always willing to help answer a quick question, process a last-minute rush order, or help out in an emergency. Thank them! Let them know you appreciate them—and let their supervisors know as well. Many organizations have internal thank-you programs—Kudos at FedEx, or The Golden Slipper award at St. Luke's Hospital, or ServUS grams at U.S. Bank. Take advantage of these opportunities to recognize your co-workers for their efforts. If you don't have a program in place, consider starting one! It's easy and inexpensive!

2. *Thank your boss.* To make sure your managers give you the support you need, give positive feedback when they help you do your job better.

3. *Thank people in other departments of your company.* While you may be the one actually talking to the customers, support people—those in warehousing, fulfillment, billing, and other departments—make the service you deliver possible. Thank them, either individually or as a group.

4. *Thank your vendors.* Without their professionalism, your customers wouldn't be receiving the satisfying service you're able to provide.

5. *Thank yourself!* You do a tough, emotionally taxing job and deserve a pat on the back. Give yourself credit for a job well done. And take yourself out for an extra special reward once in a while.

TIP: The most effective thank-yous are immediate, specific, sincere, and special.

"Gratitude is not only the greatest virtue but the mother of all the rest."

—Cicero

IV

The Problem-Solving Side of Knock Your Socks Off Service

Things don't always work out right. It's simply the law of averages. No matter how hard you try for perfection, sometimes you make a mistake. Sometimes your customer is wrong. And sometimes you just find yourself dealing with a difficult or irrational individual—someone who is never satisfied and tests your patience as well as your skills.

When things go wrong, it's time to play your trump card—your Knock Your Socks Off Service problem-solving skills. Being able to solve problems—to rescue the situation when it appears bleakest—is a key element in providing great service. It makes your job easier. It makes your company's business run smoother. And it's also a tremendous way to mend relationships with your customers and make them even more loyal.

145

27

Be a Fantastic Fixer

"Customers don't expect you to be perfect. They do expect you to fix things when they go wrong."

—Donald Porter
British Airways

You go into your wireless carrier to pick up the newest 4G model; the just-released model is sold out and won't be back in stock for at least three months. You are disappointed—even angry. *Why did they advertise it if they didn't have it?* you ask yourself. A salesperson notices your obvious upset. Maybe it's the expression on your face—or the steam coming out of your ears.

Salesperson: May I help you?

You *(grumpily):* I doubt it. I came in to upgrade to the new phone you're advertising as being released today, but surprise, surprise, you're out!

Salesperson: I'm sorry. Demand for this new model has far exceeded our expectations. We had a waiting list before we got our initial supply in the store. It will be awhile before production can catch up with all the requests, so it could be about three months before we get them back in stock.

You: Oh, great. I've just arranged to cancel my current carrier in order to get this model—what am I supposed to do for the next three months! Now, I've got nothing!

Salesperson: Wow! That's a difficult situation and I can see that you're frustrated. Here's what I can do! I can offer you a lower-cost phone at no charge—provided you maintain a 2-year contract with us—and then when the new models are back in stock, we can upgrade you at that time. Would that solution work—at least temporarily?

You agree, knowing that the benefits of the new phone far surpass the options your old phone offered, and still eager to get the newest 4G option as soon as possible.

The Art and Impact of Service Recovery

The word *recovery* means to "return to normal"—to get things back in balance or good health. That's what the store's sales associate just did for the upset would-be phone buyer. In service, good recovery begins when you recognize (and the sooner the better) that a customer has a problem.

Being a Fantastic Fixer, a real Knock Your Socks Off Service problem-solving professional, involves taking thoughtful, positive actions that will lead disappointed customers back to a state of satisfaction with your organization. Healing injured customer feelings requires sensitivity to their needs, wants, and expectations.

According to research by Fred Reichheld, the bottom-line calculation is that by focusing on customer retention tactics such as service recovery and increasing customer retention by a mere 5 percent, an organization can boost profits by up to 75 percent. (*The Ultimate Question*, Harvard Business Press, 2006)

> **TIP:** Problems exist when the customer says they do—anytime the customer is upset, dismayed, angered, or disappointed. And what constitutes a disappointment for one customer can be absolutely "no problem" for another. No matter. You can't wish (or order) a problem away because it is something no reasonable person would be upset about, because it's not your or your company's fault, or even because the customer made a mistake. If the customer <u>thinks</u> it's a problem—it's a problem.

The Recovery Process

Once a customer problem is identified, the service recovery process should begin. Not all of the six steps described below are needed for all customers. Use what you know about your company's products and services, and what you can discover about your customers' problems, to customize your actions to the specific situation. One size doesn't fit all.

1. *Apologize.* It doesn't matter who's at fault. Customers want someone to acknowledge that a problem occurred and show concern over their disappointment. Saying, "I'm sorry you have been inconvenienced this way" doesn't cost a dime, but it buys a barrel of forgiveness. Keeping the focus on the customer is not an admission to fault or ownership.

2. *Listen and empathize.* Treat your customers in a way that shows you care about them as well as about their problem. People have feelings and emotions. They want the personal side of the transaction acknowledged.

3. *Fix the problem quickly and fairly.* A "fair fix" is one that's delivered with a sense of professional concern. When all is said and done, customers want what they expected to receive in the first place, and the sooner the better.

4. *Offer atonement.* It's not uncommon for dissatisfied customers to feel injured or put out by a service

breakdown. Often they will look to you to provide some value-added gesture that says, in a manner appropriate to the problem, "I want to make it up to you."

NOTE: Atonement is not a requirement for successful recovery from every service or product breakdown. Rather, atonement is critical to satisfaction when the customer feels "injured" by the service delivery breakdown or when the customer feels victimized, greatly inconvenienced, or somehow damaged by the problem.

5. *Keep your promises.* Service recovery is needed because a customer believes a service promise has been broken. A product hasn't arrived. A call-back hasn't occurred as promised. During the recovery process, you will often need to make new promises. When you do, be realistic about what you can and can't deliver.

TIP: Take immediate steps to solve problems. The sense of urgency you bring to problem solving tells your customers that recovery is every bit as important to you (and your organization) as the initial sale.

6. *Follow up.* You can add a pleasant "extra" to the recovery sequence by following up a few hours, days, or weeks later to make sure things really were resolved to your customer's satisfaction. Following up takes little time but has a big impact on customer loyalty—and can help set you apart from the competition. Don't assume you've fixed the person or the problem. Check to be sure.

Asking for Trouble

Rather than focusing on fixing things that go wrong, shouldn't we be putting more energy into doing things right the first

Figure 27-1.

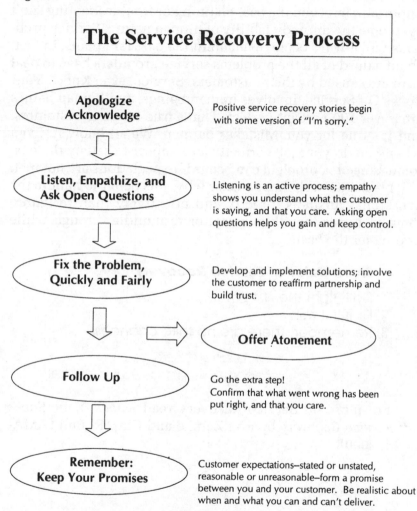

The Service Recovery Process

Apologize Acknowledge

Positive service recovery stories begin with some version of "I'm sorry."

Listen, Empathize, and Ask Open Questions

Listening is an active process; empathy shows you understand what the customer is saying, and that you care. Asking open questions helps you gain and keep control.

Fix the Problem, Quickly and Fairly

Develop and implement solutions; involve the customer to reaffirm partnership and build trust.

Offer Atonement

Follow Up

Go the extra step!
Confirm that what went wrong has been put right, and that you care.

Remember: Keep Your Promises

Customer expectations—stated or unstated, reasonable or unreasonable—form a promise between you and your customer. Be realistic about when and what you can and can't deliver.

Each episode of service breakdown is different. Sometimes you will need to use all six service-recovery steps, at other times only a few. How you use the recovery process will depend on the emotions of your customer and on the specifics of the individual situation. Only you are in a position to evaluate and act.

time? Examining the root cause of service breakdowns is important, but even the best planning or troubleshooting can't overcome the unpredictability of human nature. Service problems will always occur, even amid the best-laid plans. In fact, about a third of all the problems service providers have to deal with are caused by their customers. Service, even Knock Your Socks Off Service, involves human beings, and human beings are never 100 percent perfect. That's true for your customers, and it's true for you. Mistakes happen. We all know it. Even when you do your job correctly and appear to satisfy the customer's need, a problem can occur if expectations are not met.

No matter what happens, or why, it is better to handle the occasional mishaps directly and effectively than to ignore them in hopes they'll go away, or to muddle through while hoping for the best.

Three Rules of Service Recovery

1. Do it right the first time.
2. Fix it if it fails.
3. Remember: There are no third chances.

—Dr. Leonard Berry
Researcher, Texas A&M University

For more on Service Recovery read *Knock Your Socks Off Service Recovery* by Ron Zemke and Chip R. Bell (AMACOM, 2000).

28

The Axioms of Service Recovery

"Customers with problems have to go through a healing process before they can move on. The goal is to get the customer to say, "I'm really not happy about what happened, but I can't thank you enough for the support you provided to get me through it."

—Leo Colborne
Vice President, Global Tech Support
EMC Corporation

Customers have recovery expectations, just as they have expectations of normal service. Some of those are easy to guess at: Fix the problem, be quick about it, and show a little empathy for my inconvenience. Other customer expectations are less obvious and more subtle.

The six-step process of Chapter 27 rests on five axioms—five basic ideas about recovery—that come from what experts tell us customers expect of service recovery and our own research on the topic.

Axiom 1: Customers Have Specific Recovery Expectations

Research done in the retail banking industry by Linda Cooper of Cooper and Associates, Evanston, Illinois, found ten expectations of recovery. These ten expectations could just as easily apply to service recovery situations in many other industries as well. See Table 28-1.

Table 28-1.

TOP TEN SERVICE EXPECTATIONS OF BANK RETAIL CUSTOMERS
1. Being called back when promised.
2. Receiving an explanation of how a problem happened.
3. Knowing who to contact with a problem.
4. Being contacted promptly when a problem is resolved.
5. Being allowed to talk to someone in authority.
6. Being told how long it will take to resolve a problem.
7. Being given useful alternatives if a problem can't be solved.
8. Being treated like a person, not an account number.
9. Being told about ways to prevent a future problem.
10. Being given progress reports if a problem can't be solved immediately.

Axiom 2: Successful Recovery is Psychological as Well as Physical: Fix the Person, Then the Problem

As we have said, customers who have a problem with your product or service expect you to solve the problem. Just as important, but more difficult for customers to articulate, is the need to be "fixed" psychologically. Often a customer who has a bad experience with your company loses faith in your reliability—your ability to deliver what you promised. The repair person who goes straight to the copier or laser printer, completes the repair task, and quietly leaves for the next call may be practicing good technical service, but not good recovery. The employee who needed to use the broken machine and reported the problem needs to be "repaired" as well. If nothing more, the service person needs to give the customer an opportunity to vent his or her pent-up frustration. It's part of the job.

It is important to let customers say their piece and reassure them that everything will be fine <u>before</u> plunging into the job of fixing the problem. The most important "customer-fixing" skill you can develop is listening. Letting the customers tell their tale, blow off steam, and give you their point of view. Adding a sincere apology to the formula goes a long way toward creating a psychological fix.

Axiom 3: Work in a Spirit of Partnership

Our research suggests strongly that customers who participate in the problem-solving effort are more satisfied with the problem resolution. There are, however, limits and provisos to this idea. When your company has clearly caused the problem, asking the customer what he or she would like to see happen next gives the customer a sense of regaining control. That restored feeling of control can be vital to calming customers who believe that the organization treated them unjustly or in some way abused them, or are bordering on a perception that they have been victimized or treated unfairly.

When the customer clearly caused the problem, asking him or her to do something to help solve the problem is appropriate and increases the probability that the customer will feel satisfied with the solution. The solution, in both situations, becomes "our" solution—one we create together and both own—not "your" solution, or something you devised and are trying to impose upon the customer.

Critical to creating a sense of partnership is the way you invite the customer into the problem-solving process. The query, "So, what do you want me to do about it?" delivered in the wrong way can be seen as shifting your responsibility for service recovery back onto the customer. Better to ask, "How can we best resolve the problem?"

Remember those old movies when the doctor sends the father to off to "boil water" in preparation for a home birth? By and large, the water boiling assignment was a way of keeping the father out of the way, occupied, and feeling a part of the process. Even if all the customer can really do, metaphorically speaking, is to boil water, the effort has palliative effects.

The bank customer who failed to endorse her paycheck when she deposited it, and thereby caused a string of bounced checks, feels better about the recovery effort when given a part in fixing the problem. An assignment like "Give me a list of all the people you've written checks to" or "call the people you've written checks to and ask them to resubmit them for payment" gives the customer back some sense of psychological control.

Axiom 4: Customers React More Strongly to "Fairness" Failures Than to "Honest Mistakes"

Researcher Kathleen Seiders of Babson College in Wellesley, Massachusetts,[*] has found that when customers believe they have been treated unfairly, their reactions tend to be immediate, emotional, and enduring. In other words, if the customer feels he or she has been shortchanged, somehow manipulated, or disrespected on purpose, the reaction is heated and long lasting.

There is but one course of action for you to take when the customer feels treated unfairly—extreme apology and atonement. Sure, the customer's feelings may indeed be the result of a misunderstanding of something you or co-workers said. That is irrelevant. Once a customer feels unfairly treated, you are dealing with an at-risk customer, one in grave danger of taking his or her business elsewhere—and then telling everyone within earshot or mouse click about their bad experience with your company.

According to Dr. Seiders, communication (explaining what went wrong) and compensation (some form of atonement) can repair a perception of unfairness. It is important, she adds, to cast the explanation in terms that do not attempt to put the full responsibility for the faux pas on the shoulders of a third party or a "misunderstanding." The direct, simple, "I'm sorry this has

---

[*] Seiders, Kathleen and Leonard Berry, "Service Fairness: What It Is and Why It Matters," Academy *of Management Executive*, 1999, Volume 12, No. 2. P. 8–20.

occurred and I'll make sure it is cleared up right away" is as close to a magic bullet as there is in service recovery.

Axiom 5: Effective Recovery Is a Planned Process

Airlines and hotels overbook. Trains and planes have weather delays and cancellations so they plan ahead for these problems. If uncontrollable conditions can cause problems for your customers, creating a plan makes good sense. However, you must institute and apply the plan in a highly responsive, customer-sensitive fashion. Customers remember uncaring, robotic recovery long after they forget the incident that necessitated the solution.

It is important to know what your organization's planned recovery process looks like—if there is one. If you are creating your own planned recovery, be sure to get input and agreement from others on your team—including your boss. It is also critically important that they regularly practice implementing the plan. Customers remember two things from well-designed and

well-executed planned recovery: the quality of the solutions offered and the skill of the people offering it. Of the two, the skill
of the people delivering the solution has the bigger impact on
customers. What skills are those? We've conducted over 90 focus groups over the years and asked them, "what makes for a
positive recovery experience?" The ten most memorable service
representative actions they experienced are listed in Table 28-2.

Table 28-2.

What Focus Group Members Remembered and Found Impressive	% of Interviewees Who Commented on and Were Impressed by This Action
CSR dealt with my upset	79.0%
CSR apologized	69.1%
CSR didn't become defensive, but showed humility and poise	62.9%
CSR followed up after the complaint transaction	56.8%
CSR showed skill at problem solving	53.0%
CSR, when appropriate, was proactive in admitting organization error, didn't try to shift blame	44.4%
CSR acted in a fully responsible and empowered fashion on the customer's behalf	40.7%
CSR showed good interpersonal skills, particularly listening	40.7%
CSR showed empathy for the customer's plight and/or upset	38.3%
CSR believed the customer, valued the customer's perception	24.7%

We know that recovery is about both fixing the problem and fixing the person. In looking at these memorable service actions, that's why we say repeatedly, "Fix the person first; then fix the problem."

"You can't guarantee you'll never make mistakes. You can guarantee you'll fix them."

—Jeff Bezos, Founder and CEO, Amazon.com

29

Use the Well-Placed "I'm Sorry"

"A few words of regret is a way of saying you care, a show of sensitivity to the ragged edges of another's emotion."

—Robert Conklin
How to Get People to Do Things

The words are so simple—"I'm sorry"—yet we hear them far too infrequently. In fact, our research shows that when customers tell a company about a problem with a product or service, they receive an apology less than half the time. That's about half as often as they should. The solution to every problem, whether major or minor, should start with a sincere apology.

Why is it so hard for us to say "I'm sorry" to our customers? First and foremost, we may be intimidated by the words. We may think that "I'm sorry" actually means "I've failed," "I'm not a good person," or "I'm not professional." Nothing could be further from the truth. An apology is simply an acknowledgment that things aren't going right in your customer's eyes.

Legal Jeopardy

Today, there is also a tendency to equate being sorry with an admission of personal or corporate liability—that being sorry means you are somehow to blame. Viral videos or megabuck lawsuits are common stories from YouTube to cable news shows to prime-time entertainment programs. It's understand-

160

able that companies worry about the potential financial consequences of an apology and individuals are reluctant to take the blame personally.

If your job has legal or regulatory aspects, make sure you understand what they are and how they affect what you do. But don't assume that you're not allowed to say, "I'm sorry you were inconvenienced," when a snafu occurs. Actually, a sincere apology delivered in a timely and professional manner often goes a long way toward heading off potential legal problems. When you show your willingness to make sure your customers receive what they expect to receive, you relieve them of the need to even think about starting a fight.

Customer Jeopardy

Just as apologizing is not an admission of responsibility ("I'm sorry *we* did this to you"), neither is it an opportunity to place blame ("I'm sorry *you* were too stupid to read the directions before turning it on and shorting it out").

We all know that customers don't always use their own common sense or the painstakingly detailed directions we give them. Sometimes, for whatever the reason, they do it

wrong—with predictably disastrous consequences. They look to us to fix it. And since no one likes to admit a mistake, they'll often blame us in the process.

> **TIP:** A sincere apology is a personal and professional acknowledgment that your customer was disappointed or inconvenienced. When saying the words "I'm sorry" feels like taking on too much of the blame, consider saying "Thank you for bringing that to my attention," instead.

When a customer of Buckner Inc., a Fresno, California–based irrigation products company, sent back a couple of the company's brass sprinkler heads for repair, employees didn't think much of it. That is, until they discovered the sprinklers were of the fossil variety—antique models manufactured in 1948 that were long obsolete.

Buckner no longer makes sprinklers the same way, with leather washers, and did not have the parts needed for repair. But the customer had grown attached to the hardware over the years and didn't want the offered replacements. According to the *Fresno Bee*, the sprinkler heads had been in the customer's family for three generations.

So Tony Garcia, a Buckner employee, took the sprinkler heads home over one weekend and fashioned some new leather washers from an old pair of shoes, then sent the sprinklers back to the customer—without charge. The customer, delighted beyond words, insisted on learning who had done the work and sent Garcia a check to cover his labor.

Did Garcia have to make the extra effort to help this customer? Of course not. But the customer—and the many others who heard him gleefully retell the story or who read about the episode in the *Fresno Bee*—heard the message loud and clear: We'll do whatever it takes to satisfy a customer.

Scapegoating

When things go wrong, there's an almost instinctive urge to direct the customer's attention elsewhere: "If those 'smart guys' in information technology could ever figure out how to make this computer system work the way it's supposed to, we wouldn't have to put you through long waits like this," or "Maintenance was supposed to clean that up last night, but I guess they were too busy taking a coffee break. So you ended up stepping in it."

TIP: Scapegoating another part of your organization for a service breakdown simply tells your customers that you're separate departments working in isolated and even adversarial ways, instead of a tight-knit team working for them. Don't do it—not to each other, not to yourself.

Do It Right

A vague apology delivered in an impersonal, machinelike manner can be worse than no apology at all. Effective apologies are:

1. *Sincere.* While you may not know exactly what your customers are feeling and experiencing individually, you can be genuine in your concern.
2. *Personal.* Apologies are far more powerful when they are delivered in the first person: "*I* am sorry that you are experiencing a problem." Remember, to the customer, you—not some mysterious "we" or "they"—are the company.
3. *Timely.* Don't wait to find out why there is a problem or what caused it before expressing regret that the problem exists in the first place. The sooner you react to a distressed customer, the better.

"I believe that if you are honest and straightforward with customers, they will treat you like a neighbor when circumstances beyond your control put you in a 'one-down' position."

—Milton Moore
General Manager, Vision Cable

30
Fix the Person

"Here's your food and I hope you choke on it!!"
—Fast-food server to a customer who complained
about waiting ten minutes to be served.
(*We're not making it up.*)

The toughest part of dealing with people, as you already know, is dealing with people. When products develop problems, customers have an object to curse, kick, yell at, and focus their feelings on. When a service breaks down, on the other hand, the focus of their emotional reaction is on you.

According to a 2005 study, upset customers aren't just getting mad these days, more are out to get even. The report, conducted by the Customer Care Alliance in collaboration with the Arizona State University School of Business, found that 70 percent of 1,012 survey respondents experienced "customer rage" as a result of recent service encounters. Some 15 percent of those who received poor service actually sought some form of revenge for their pain and frustration (the good news is only one percent reported acting on the urge) and 13 percent said they used profanity when interacting with service providers. Global management consulting firm Accenture found in their *Customer Satisfaction Survey* (2008) that 52 percent of respondents said that their expectations for customer service were higher than in the period five years before. In addition, 67 percent of respondents reported taking their business elsewhere as a result of shoddy service during the previous year.

It is tempting to respond in kind to the emotional fireworks set off by disgruntled customers. Tempting, but not very wise, and certainly not very productive. Meeting anger with anger, sarcasm with sarcasm, frustration with impatience, or ignoring the emotional element altogether leaves both server and served feeling badly bruised. And understandably, neither may be anxious for a repeat performance. Knock Your Socks Off Service professionals recognize the emotional element of a service breakdown, and manage the recovery in a calm, professional, even-tempered way. To do that, it's not enough to just fix the problem. You also have to fix the person.

Color-Coding Your Response

Just as problems will have different solutions, fixing the person takes a different form depending on the "color" of your customer's emotional state. As a service professional, you've probably encountered it all, from coldly angry to frothing at the mouth. Some people seem very understanding when things go wrong, some make you feel absolutely terrible for playing a role in a service snafu, and others can instill a very real sense of fear in you.

We find it helpful to group upset customers into three emotional colors: Blasé Blue, Ornery Orange, and Raging Red.

- *Blasé Blue Customers.* These customers don't give you enough emotional clues to decipher their level of upset. For some, the service breakdown may simply be a nonemotional event—they roll with the punch and don't let it bother them. But be aware that seemingly neutral customers can move up the emotional scale if you don't take their concerns seriously.
- *Ornery Orange Customers.* Annoyed, these people exhibit mild irritation because their experience has fallen short of their expectations. Take them lightly or refuse to acknowledge their upset however and you can quickly escalate them to four-alarm fire status. Handle with care.
- *Raging Red Customers.* These customers have major feelings of ire and frustration; they feel victimized and

hurt by the service breakdown. Usually you won't have any trouble identifying their level of concern—it will be obvious to everyone within a three-block radius.

To see the differences among the three, consider these re-actions to essentially the same initial situation, a late airplane flight:

Blasé Blue: Bob's flight arrives one hour late, but he had a ninety-minute layover and can still make his next con-nection, so Bob's plans haven't been affected.

Ornery Orange: Olivia's flight is one hour late, causing her to miss a connection and to have to re-book on a later flight.

Raging Red: Ray's flight is one hour late, causing him to miss the last connection, resulting in an unplanned overnight stay and the need to call and reschedule a full day's worth of appointments.

Knowing the emotional color of your customer will help you choose the best people-fixing techniques. Here's a handy guide. If your customer is:

Blasé Blue

- Show surprise
- Use general people-handling skills
- Key into the customer

Ornery Orange

- Show urgency
- Enlist the customer in generating solutions
- Create added value by offering something extra to atone for the problem

Raging Red

- Show empathy
- Allow venting
- Create calm
- Listen actively
- Plan follow-up

Real problem solving cannot happen until the issues are out on the table. Blasé Blue customers often seem calm while "testing" your response. Show surprise and you demonstrate that this is not "business as usual"—and you pass the test. Fail to use good people handling skills and watch this calm customer jump to Raging Red status. The tactics for Ornery Orange are designed to give this customer back a feeling of control and importance. Orneriness is often a substitute for fear or discomfort. Raging Red needs to be coaxed out of a temper tantrum.

Tip of the Iceberg

Fixing the person is an important element of a well-conceived recovery effort because many times a customer's emotional reaction is only tangentially tied to the real service problem. When you encounter an upset customer, you can't tell from the initial emotional readout whether their problem stems from a late flight, a broken radiator, a bounced check, or even, well . . . consider this illustration:

A friend of ours spent some years working behind the counter of an ice cream store. One very busy day, a business-man came in and ordered a banana split. She made it, handed it to him, and went on to the next customer. Moments later, the customer was back. "This banana split has no bananas!" he hollered. "What kind of a moron makes a banana split with no bananas!!"

Stunned by the outburst, our friend could do little more than look at the man—and at the banana-less split. When he finally paused for a breath, she made the necessary effort: "Gee, I'm awfully sorry about that. No bananas is a pretty se-rious offense in a banana split. I think I'd be upset, too. Please, let me make you a fresh one—and refund your money."

About that time, the customer became aware that he was ranting and raving over a bowl of ice cream, under the stares of the other customers and confronted by nothing more threat-ening than the sincere concern on a young woman's face. He started laughing. And she started to smile. And the other customers started to giggle and laugh. The upshot was that while she was making the new banana split, he apologized to her. And, perhaps needless to say, continued to be a regular customer at that ice cream shop.

> "When a service tech goes on site, he has two repairs: He has to fix the equipment and fix the cus-tomer. And fixing the customer is more important."
>
> —Bill Bleuel
> Customer Satisfaction Consultant

31
Fair-Fix the Problem

"If you have trouble, it reduces the likelihood that the person is going to buy the next time."

—Joseph M. Juran
Founder of the Quality Movement

Have you noticed that some people just seem naturally good at problem solving? No matter what the situation, no matter what the conflict, they are always able to see some course of action that will get the job done. Perhaps you are one of those people.

If you aren't, you may think, "I'll never be able to be as effective as they are—I don't have the talent." Wrong. Problem-solving is a skill, not a talent. Effective problem solvers have simply learned to use their skills. To practice and hone your problem-solving skills, we recommend using a three-step framework: Listen—Probe—Solve.

Step 1: LISTEN to Find the Problem

The importance of good listening cannot be overstated. In a problem-solving situation, you are listening for two reasons:

1. To allow your customers to vent their frustration or irritation—part of the "fix the person" process.
2. To find the real problem (which may be obvious, but sometimes isn't).

For example, "listen" to this customer's complaint:

"I bought a Kid-Pro Bike from you people last night.
The box must have weighed eighty pounds! I finally
got it into my car—no help from you guys—and
home, and it took me an hour to get it out of the car,
into the house, and open. I mean really! This is a
kid's bike and you need Arnold Schwarzenegger to
open the box! And after all that, the directions were
missing! How am I supposed to put it together without the directions?!"

TIP: Your customer has been practicing her little
speech all the way to your store or office—don't
deprive her of the right to deliver it, and in as dramatic a fashion as she likes. Even if you're sure you
understand the problem—don't interrupt. You
may be right, but you may not be. Listen until your
customer is done explaining. She'll feel better for
getting the whole story off her chest, and you may
discover pieces of the puzzle you didn't even know
were missing.

Upset customers are apt to bring multiple issues into their
tirade. It's important to this customer that she had difficulty
getting the box from the store to her car and then into her
house. But the immediate problem is the missing directions.

Step 2: PROBE for Understanding and Confirmation

Customers, particularly upset customers, don't always explain everything clearly or completely. Ask questions about
anything you may not understand or need clarified. Then,
when you feel you have identified and clearly grasped the
problem, repeat it back to the customer.
    "I'm concerned about your purchase experience, and I'm
going to share that with our manager. What I understand you

need right now is directions. I've had that problem with assembling things myself—parts everywhere, with no directions in sight—and I know how frustrating it can be."

> **TIP:** Use this step to make it clear that you agree that what the customer says is a problem really is a problem. Nothing annoys customers more than to hear a service representative respond to their concerns with an offhand "So?"

STEP 3: Find and Implement SOLUTIONS

If the problem is one that you have encountered before, you may already know the best solution. In that case, use the "feel, felt, found" approach to present it:

> "I can understand that you feel _____. Other people, including myself, have felt the same way. We've found that _____ solves the problem."

When the best solution is less obvious, present several options and ask for the customer's preferences.

> "Fortunately, this doesn't happen very often. In those few cases when it does, I've found a few solutions that work. One is to check in the stockroom to see if we have another carton with a set of instructions in it. Or, if you're in more of a hurry, I can make a photocopy or scan the master copy we have and fax or e-mail it to you. Which works best for you?"

Involving customers in generating solutions not only starts to rebuild the relationship, it gives them the feeling that your business really is interested in satisfying their needs. You'll find that most customers bring a sense of fair play with them and will often expect far less than you'd think. In our research into telephone repair services, for example, we learned that customers who experienced problems on the weekend

didn't expect immediate service. They reasoned that telephone repair technicians wanted to spend weekend time with their own families, just like customers.

TIP: If the solution you suggest is rejected by your customer, or is met with a lukewarm reception, you may not be solving the real problem. Keep probing by asking what else your customer would like to see happen.

One Extra Step

Sometimes, solving the actual problem is not quite enough. Remember that the purpose of a Fantastic Fix isn't only to correct the problem, but also—perhaps more importantly—to keep the customer. Rebuilding a damaged relationship, particularly when a customer feels victimized by the service breakdown, may require taking an extra step we call "symbolic atonement." It means making an appropriate gesture that says, "I want to make it up to you." Atonement is a way of providing a value-added touch to tell customers their business is important to you:

"I'm glad you gave us a chance to make things right. Before you leave, let me write our store phone number on the assembly directions. And since you had to make an extra trip, I'd like to give you one of these personalized bike license plates. What's your son's name?"

"Don't fight, make it right."

—Hardee's complaint-handling policy

32

Service Recovery in the Digital Age

"Why should I wait longer for an Internet web site than
I do for a McDonald's drive-through order?"

—Anonymous

No talk of service recovery is complete without mentioning the challenges presented by serving customers over the Internet. Consumers and businesses continue to flock to the Internet to buy products and services, lured by the ease of comparison shopping and the convenience of transacting business over the computer rather than traveling to the local mall.

But plenty of those e-tailers and "click and brick" companies—organizations with both stores and Internet sales sites—are still focused only on acquiring customers, not servicing them. Having an aesthetically pleasing web site is one thing, creating the customer support, online problem help, and other shopper-friendly features needed to keep e-shoppers coming back beyond one visit is quite another. That raises the stakes for good service recovery online—and that's where you come in. Experts agree that the standard for customer service and problem solving is higher for the web than it is in the offline, face-to-face customer service world. Why? Because customers think of the Internet and the computers that drive it as fast and easy and expect the service they receive over the Internet to be fast and easy.

Online shoppers start out with high expectations of the cyber-shopping experience. Customers who can shop around

174

the clock on the Internet now expect round-the-clock service; something they'd never think of demanding from a store. When they visit web sites and find online chat features or send out e-mail requests for help or more information, many expect a response instantly or at least within an hour or two—not realizing or caring that the service rep on the receiving end might be juggling requests from hundreds of other customers at the same time.

Companies in the e-commerce business need to proactively deal with a new strain of customer complaint: The "cybervent" or the complaint lodged via e-mail, Twitter, YouTube, Facebook or other social media, or by bloggers taking companies to task on their web sites. No longer can organizations sit back and wait for complaints to slowly filter by their desks. Instead, they must actively pursue them—a quick Google search or a search on social media search engines such as socialmention.com on a daily or every-other-day basis will work wonders to soothe an anxious mind. The growing presence of influential customers hitting the Net has forced many companies to begin actively monitoring these sites—or to hire contractors to track the commentary for them—to gauge customer reaction to their brands and respond to tales of poor service that often spread like wildfire on the Internet, doing considerable damage to corporate reputations.

Consider this recent case. When flying on a United Airlines flight, musician Dave Carroll checked his guitar through baggage. While awaiting departure, his seatmate pointed out that the baggage handlers were having a great time tossing around a musical instrument. You got it. It was Dave's guitar. Upon retrieving his guitar at his final destination, Dave discovered it was broken. When United didn't respond to repeated requests for some remuneration, he resorted to producing a video and putting it on YouTube. One year later, the video has had over 10 million hits. The story hit the national airwaves and many national publications. Can your company afford such attention? This story has a happy ending: United hired Dave Carroll to help them learn how to do a better job of dealing with customer complaints. But that's seldom the outcome.

Unhappy Internet customers find the detached distance of e-mail or blogs a license to complain more regularly—and often with more emotional fervor and in a nastier tone.

Preliminary Rules of the Road

While the rules for Internet service are always evolving, there are some emerging guidelines. Here are a few simple ideas your organization should be looking at to improve its e-service and reduce the number of recovery situations it has to deal with:

- *Easy Customer Access to Phone Numbers.* Far too many web sites don't list a phone number, or the number is difficult to locate. There should be an 800 number on your company's home page that is easy for e-customers to find—and someone at that number to help them when they call. Take a look. If you don't see one or it isn't easy to find, bring that to someone's attention. If customers tell you the phone number was hard to find, report that as well.
- *One-Click Help.* Help for customers—whether it involves product availability, billing, order confirmation, delivery tracking, or other information—should never

be more than one click away. Customers should not be forced to click endlessly into carpal tunnel trauma to find what they need. If the customer can easily find these things on your web site, they are less likely to call you for that information. Many organizations have added an instant chat function to their web sites to increase customer interaction and one-click help. Go explore your company's web site. If it takes more than four clicks to find customer service and send a message, report that. If customers tell you they hate all the clicking they have to do—report that as well.

- *A List of Frequently Asked Questions (FAQs).* Well-conceived and clearly written FAQs take the pressure off live phone or online (e-mail) support by giving customers easy and around-the-clock access to the most commonly asked questions about your company. Some experts advise creating two layers of FAQs—one for prospective or new customers with fundamental questions, and another for continuing customers who are familiar with your products or services. Look your company's FAQs over. If the questions you find yourself answering most frequently for customers are not in the FAQ, report that. If customers tell you the answers in the FAQ aren't clear, report that as well.

- *Standards for E-Mail Response.* There should be clear, set standards for response time to e-mail inquiries and clear guidelines for answering questions and addressing problems in customer-sensitive ways.

- *Removing Pre-Sale Registration Requirements.* A recent study by customer research firm Vividence Corp. of customers using 17 popular web shopping sites found shoppers' biggest frustration was being forced to go through a registration process before making a purchase. There are few things as rage-inducing as spending time researching products on a web site, filling a check-out cart with items, and then being told you have to complete a lengthy registration form before the site can process your transaction. It's a primary reason why some sites experience abnormally high cart-abandonment rates.

The web is an immediate medium, and long delays in response times can dull customer loyalty. Once a customer has been disappointed by how slowly questions are answered or problems resolved, they're not likely to try again. Because of the increased use of Twitter, Best Buy developed their Twelpforce to offer immediate—and we mean immediate—assistance for customer questions, concerns, or ideas. Customers compare that immediate response with the time it takes you to respond via e-mail.

> **TIP:** Lands' End receives about 400 e-mail requests daily, and staffers have a standard of responding within three hours. At Dell Computer, support technicians answer most customer e-mails within four hours. How do your company's standards measure up?

In the spirit of keeping online customers apprised and updated of your work on their behalf, there should be some form of "auto acknowledgment," a computer program that responds to customers' incoming e-mail requests, stating that the question was received and sending back a response estimating how long it will take to answer the question. If your company doesn't have one, ask why not.

Check your own site's registration process, and if requires first-time customers to register before making a purchase (rather than after the sale or when they're repeat customers) ask someone why the company is content to drive valuable business away—and create damaging word of mouth from aggrieved customers.

- *Product return channels are synchronized and complement each other.* Customers are none too pleased when they order products from a web site only to find that they can't return it at the company's brick-and-mortar store. Zappos.com, the online shoe/clothing/accessory and more site, not only ships items overnight, but pays for the shipping if a return is needed. They decided that service is their differentiator and supports that with synchronized processes. Are your company's Internet return policies synchronized for easy in-person product return? If they aren't, you need to know why and what the two different systems are, because your customers will surely want to know.

"Desert your online customers and they'll return the favor."

—www.liveperson.com

33

Recovery: Social Media Style

"The road to online success is paved with the short sighted, the slow and the unprepared."

—Gordon Brooks,
President and CEO, Breakaway Solutions

"You mean we have to be prepared for service recovery in social media, too?" Yep! It's true. Now, more than ever, your customers are looking for ways to reach you to resolve their service breakdowns quickly and effectively. It's your job as a Knock Your Socks Off Service professional to "fix it" wherever they are. That means wherever they're going to find assistance, you'd better be there ready to make it right!

Kate Ryan, one of the contributors to the Tech Affect Blog, relates the following Twitter encounter in a recent column.

"I was checking my e-mail when it happened." The dreaded cancellation notice of an online purchase from Best Buy, just minutes before I was heading out to pick up the new flat screen TV I ordered for in-store pick-up. I was extremely frustrated, so I went to Twitter to make it public that my TV had been canceled—and all I got from a Best Buy representative on Twitter was a note to call 1-888-BESTBUY:

@kateryanNY I can imagine that would be horrible. I'd call 888-BESTBUY. They should be able to get things sorted out. #twelpforce
2:59 PM Dec 5th, 2010 via web in reply to kateryanNY

While that made me cranky, I was even crankier the next night when I received an e-mail from the store's corporate division: "Just a friendly pick-up reminder for your purchase!" Wait, a pick-up reminder for a canceled TV? Noting that the charge was still reflected on my credit card, I immediately dialed their customer service number. Patiently, I sat through selecting an option, listening to musical interludes, and being assured by a recording that I was the next caller. An hour of waiting on hold later, without ever being connected to a human being, I hung up—about ready to scream.

That's when I went to Twitter, once more:

BEYOND angry w/ @bestbuy. Canceled my order yesterday, then sent me a "pickup reminder" today. Still no refund. #FAIL #twelpforce
9:13 PM Dec 6th, 2010 via web

"After waiting an hour on the phone with their customer service, I wasn't expecting much from their *#twelpforce*. But within a few minutes, @jayysenn, a Best Buy rep, responded directly to my tweet, asking if there was anything he could help with. In the matter of just one more tweet, @jayysenn had asked me to e-mail my order details and customer service issue to him, and then he called me directly on my cell phone to troubleshoot. (Turns out the order had never been officially canceled, resulting in the pick-up reminder and the charges on my credit card.) On the phone, he officially canceled the order, checked on my new order, and offered me a credit for my trouble. Needless to say, I was a much happier cus-tomer—and I quickly canceled my original ban on ever shopping at the store again."

A great example! And Kate's story exemplifies both the incorrect and the correct way to connect with your angry and frustrated customers who are looking to lash out with little hope of getting a response.

Let's run Kate's story through the service recovery process and see where it excels and where it falls short.

Apologize/Acknowledge Upset

In Kate's first response, Twelpforce had the potential of knocking her socks off. Not only did they respond in about an hour, but they acknowledged her frustration and upset. But after that great start, they failed to take ownership of the problem. By passing Kate on to the toll-free number for fur-ther assistance, they passed the buck and ended up causing Kate even greater frustration. Don't ask your customer to do your work for them—instead, when you offer to help, mean it! If a customer needs to talk to someone on the phone to get the resolution they need, then offer to contact the customer directly.

Listen/Empathize and Ask Open Questions

This is a great example of a time when it would've been bene-ficial to ask Kate to further the discussion offline. Once Kate had voiced her initial frustration, a quick query asking if she'd be willing to share more information via a direct message shows followers that her situation has been acknowledged and enables you to offer Kate your full attention and to get the complete story. Caution: Be sure you're following your customer—they won't be able to contact you privately if you're not—that will cause even more frustration.

Fix the Problem

This is clearly where things went awry for Kate. The "fix" to this problem didn't happen the first time around and her mild case of frustration was suddenly escalated to the chronic stage. In one last cry for help, she again tweeted her displeasure—this time Twelpforce's @Jayysenn came to the rescue! @Jayysenn took Kate's issue offline and called her personally to discuss the situation. He took ownership, checked on her situation, and resolved it quickly and efficiently.

Offer Atonement

@Jayysenn wasn't finished with making things just right for Kate. He took it a step further and offered her a credit for her inconvenience. He wanted to ensure that she wasn't just satisfied, but that she would remain a loyal Best Buy customer. And it appears he succeeded. Kate indicated that she removed her self-imposed Best Buy ban and will more than likely be shopping there again. Not only that, but all of Kate's blog readers now know her story and that @twelpforce does mean business when it comes to taking care of its customers.

Follow-Up

We don't know if @Jayysenn followed up with Kate to make sure she received her big screen TV—Kate doesn't share that part of her story. But we'd be pretty surprised if he neglected that important step.

The service recovery process works! It works for face-to-face encounters, for upset customers over the phone, it applies to e-mails and web sites, and it most definitely has a place in social media. Learn it and make it work for you—and your customers!

> "When you realize that your customer is just like you, the whole dynamic of your interaction with them changes."
>
> —Elizabeth Spaulding, L.L. Bean, Inc.

34

Customers From Hell® Are Customers, Too

"There are no "bad" customers; some are just harder to please than others."
—Someone who never waited on a customer in his life

There is a world of difference between keeping your composure while working with an upset, angry customer who has had a bad day in Consumerland and the burning sensation you get in your stomach when you come face-to-face with a fire-breathing, show-no-mercy, take-no-prisoners Customer From Hell.

Customers who have been *through* consumer hell need your help, support, and understanding. Those who come to you direct *from* hell need the special care and handling you might give a live hand grenade or an angry rattlesnake.

You would never tell the second group to their faces what you're thinking —"Oh no! another Customer From Hell"—but there's nothing wrong with admitting to yourself that this is what working with them feels like.

Customers From Hell play a simple game. Their goal is to get under your skin, to provoke you to counterattack. They taunt. . . you react. . . they win. If you lose control, you lose everything. Often, your first impulse is either to run and hide or to smack 'em. Or both. But you can't really do either. So, what do you do?

1. Develop some perspective. Real Customers From Hell are relatively few and far between. Most of your customers want to deal with you in a cheerful, positive way. And even the really difficult ones are still human beings worthy of fair treatment.
2. Remember that you are a pro. *You* know your job and your company. *You* know your products and how they perform. And *you* know how to handle people, even when it's the end of the day, the end of the week, or the end of August and the air-conditioning is broken.
3. Be a master of the art of calm. Let the upset and anger wash over you without sticking. Angry customers are almost never mad at you personally. They are mad at a situation they don't like.

Approaches to Obnoxious Customers

Our research with customers—and your stories of dealing with the most difficult ones—suggest four steps that, applied correctly, can help calm the savage in the most beastly customer.

1. *See no evil, hear no evil.* If you start thinking of customers as jerks and idiots, before you know it you'll start treating them as badly as they treat you. Worse yet, you will start to treat the innocent like the guilty.

Mr. John Q. McNasty, a customer of the Acme Company, is the biggest jerk you have ever had to deal with. One day, you decide to fight fire with fire and be just as rude and insulting as he is. You give him a dose of his own medicine—and you feel great. John Q., of course, goes back to Acme and tells everyone what a stinker you are and that all *he* did was ask for a little service. Soon you begin to notice other Acme customers acting up when you deal with them. And then, of course, you

have to show these jerks that you can be just as tough as they are. And then. . . . You get the point, right?

Customers From Hell feed on your reactions. They use your response to justify their own behavior. Ignoring their rude and crude words and actions sends the message, "Slam, bang, and cuss all you want. I am not intimidated." And that message—demonstrated but not spoken—gives *you* the advantage.

2. *Surface the tension.* Some customers push your personal hot buttons through use of foul language or condescending tone. Others seem to direct their anger at you as if you were solely responsible for every woe in their lives. In fact, angry, temper-tantrum throwing customers are so wrapped up in their emotions they often forget that you are a living, feeling person. "Surface the tension" is a way to gently remind them. Say: "Have I done something personally to upset you? I'd like to help. Please give me a chance." This will help return the customer's focus back to the issue, encouraging him or her to vent about the problem and not the person. The tag line, "Please give me a chance" is the real magic worker. We learned it from FedEx, where agents have long realized that it is a rare customer who won't, even if grudgingly, give you a chance. And

that's often all it takes to turn a frustrated customer from irate to repentant.

TIP: Don't try your company's Ten Commandments on Customers From Hell. Quoting rules or policy to justify your actions simply gives this kind of person something concrete to scream about.

3. *Transfer transformation.* There <u>are</u> times when you are not obligated to continue a conversation with a customer. If you are personally offended, shocked, or dismayed by foul language, you have a right to deal with it. If a customer won't allow you to help him or her, you have an obligation to connect the customer to someone he or she will work with. Transferring the customer, be it to a peer or to a supervisor, is not a cop-out. Instead, it is—if used in these situations—a clever, preplanned method for moving beyond a customer's negative, nasty behavior.

TIP: Worried that a customer's answer might be "Yes, as a matter of fact you have ruined my life"? It rarely happens, but if that is the answer, it's important to know why so you can correct the problem or misperception — or simply choose to move to the next tactic.

When you use this tactic, you'll notice a strange, yet very human phenomenon. Consider what happens when Carol D. McSurly calls to inquire about a billing problem. You try to "surface the tension," but get "You imbecile! It's people like you who caused the fall of every great society! I want to talk to someone who actually has a brain!" So, take a deep breath and put her on hold. You call your supervisor and explain the situation before putting Ms. McSurly's call through. Then you hightail it to your supervisor's cubicle to watch her reaction when Ms. McSurly cuts loose. Instead, you see your supervisor smile and nod as she coos reassuring platitudes. Wait, it's worse! Your supervisor is actually laughing at something

McSurly said! As she hangs up the phone, your supervisor turns to you and says, "What a character that McSurly is! Nice woman. What did you say to upset her?"

Are McSurly and your supervisor secret psychic twins? No. McSurly was having an adult temper tantrum. In putting her on hold, you put her in adult time-out. Just like those times you might use time-out with a small child, McSurly transitioned from her time-out to a different activity—in her case, speaking to a supervisor. She was able to leave her tantrum, and her terrible talk, in the past with you and make a fresh start in this new conversation.

4. *Build contractual trust.* What if McSurly doesn't quiet down? Or worse, what if a customer threatens you or begins to push and shove? At this point, it is time to draw a line in the sand—but not one that forces your customer into the cold water of the river. Rather, you want to take your customer across a bridge and leave him or her on the far bank.

You are assistant maître d' at Chez Hot Stuff Café, the smartest, trendiest new restaurant in town. You are booked solid for the evening when Mr. McNasty arrives with three friends and no reservation. McNasty takes you by the arm, leads you aside, and tells you that you *will* seat his party immediately if you know what's good for you. All the time he is talking, he is smiling—and squeezing your upper arm in an obviously menacing way. Make positive eye contact, smile right back and say, "I'm sorry but unless we can find another way to have this conversation—a way that doesn't involve physical contact—I am going to have to call Security."

You may have to repeat this phrase a second time, and then give him a moment to realize that you are serious. Then, if he stops, offer to put him on the waiting list. If not, say, "I'm sorry we couldn't find a way to work together." Call for your manager in a firm, *loud* voice. Then call 911.

TIP: Use "I" statements like the one above. "You are a big bully who smells bad and probably has no

friends," is bound to create resentment and de-
fensiveness. "I" statements clearly communicate
that you need the customer to stop a particular
behavior — be it swearing or pushing — because,
while others may find it okay, <u>you</u> can't accept that
behavior.

Most customers will comply after you make the "Stop
this behavior and I'll help you; continue it and I won't" contract clear. If the customer doesn't comply, it's imperative
that you follow through. This builds what psychologists call
"contractual trust." In other words, you made a promise—"I'll
call Security"—and you kept it.

Which tactic is best? Any of the above four approaches
can be correct in the right situation. Talk with your peers and
talk with your manager about when and how to apply each
remedy to your difficult customers.

"The customer isn't king anymore—the customer
is dictator!"

—Anonymous

35

The Customers From Hell® Hall of Shame

"They're only puttin' in a nickel, and they want a dollar song. . . ."

—Country song lyrics

Not all customers from hell are created equal. Some are masters of the slow drum. Others are top of their lungs screamers. Some beg. Some cry. Some threaten. A few even flatter. Our advice: Know Thy Enemy!

In our view there are FIVE types of Customers From Hell®.

Egocentric Edgar

Me first, me last, me only—that's his creed. You? You're just a bit player, an extra, an extraneous piece of scenery in that grandest of all productions: "Edgar: The Greatest Story Ever Told."

Sample Behaviors

Won't wait his turn, will only speak to whomever is in charge, intimidates through judicious name dropping, and makes loud demands.

Ways to Work with Edgar

- *Appeal to his ego.* Because Edgar is already a legend in his own mind, nothing soothes him faster than being acknowledged as a VIP. Simple things like remembering his name and using it can have a major impact.
- *Demonstrate action.* Edgar really doesn't believe that you can or will do anything to help him. Taking some measurable, immediate action will go miles toward an amenable resolution of his problem—even if the problem exists only in his mind.
- *Don't talk policy.* Edgar does not want to hear about your company policy (as a matter of fact, no customer with a problem wants to hear about your company policy). Edgar expects to be exempt from any policies. Saying something like, "For you I can offer. . .," and then offer whatever your standard policy is.
- *Don't let his ego destroy yours.* Edgar can be terrifically overbearing and his superior attitude invites the customer service person to feel unimportant. Don't take his self-importance as a personal affront. Focus on the business at hand, not on Edgar's disdainfulness.

Bad Mouth Betty

Her mother would be proud. Such an extensive vocabulary! It takes timing, talent, and a total lack of shame to swear like a trooper, but Betty makes it look easy.

Sample Behaviors

Uses language and has a demeanor that is caustic, crude, cruel, and foul.

Ways to Work with Betty

- *Ignore her language.* If you let her language get to you, then you've lost. Even though four-letter words are offensive, try to block them out. Remember she's really lashing out at the organization and not at you personally. Betty can often be defanged by asking, "Excuse me, have I done something personally to offend you? Because if I have, I'd like to fix it or apologize." Betty is likely to stop in her tracks, say "no," and tell you what she's really upset about.

- *Force the issue.* If Betty is swearing a blue streak, interrupt her and say, "Excuse me, but I don't have to listen to that kind of language and I'm going to hang up right now." As soon as you do that go immediately to your supervisor and say, "I just hung up on this customer for this reason." Research shows that most of the time (about 80 percent) the customer will call back and apologize.

- *Use selective agreement.* When Betty comes to you complaining about the outrageous waiting time in the teller line, agree with her! "Five minutes is a long time to wait, I can see why you would be upset."

Hysterical Harold

He's a screamer. If it's true that there is a child in all of us yearning to break free, Harold demonstrates the dark side of that happy thought. He is the classic tantrum-thrower, the adult embodiment of the terrible twos. Only louder. Much louder.

Sample Behaviors

Screams, is rabid and extremely animated, jumps around, and invades the personal space of others.

Ways to Work with Harold

- *Let him vent.* Harold has a lot of pent-up emotion. Let him wind down. Show Harold you accept his feelings, whether or not you agree with them, with neutral statements like, "I can see that you're upset," or "I don't blame you for being angry."

- *Take it backstage.* A public area is not the ideal location for Harold to explode. Walk him to a more secluded area like a conference room or private office. However, Harold may resist, thinking he's more likely to get his way if his tantrum is on display for other customers.
- *Take responsibility for solving the problem.* After Harold finally calms down, find out what the real problem is. Let him know that you want to and will do whatever you can to solve it.

Dictatorial Dick

Dick often shows up with marching orders. He issues ultimatums, sets arbitrary deadlines, and tells everyone exactly how to do their jobs—after all, he "used to be in the business." And when his plan doesn't work? It's your company's fault, of course. Better still, it's your fault.

Sample Behaviors

Shows up with multiple copies of written directions or orders, insists on doing things his way, and suspects sabotage if things don't go his way.

Ways to Work with Dick

Break up his game. Dick believes that getting adequate service from an organization requires going to war and striking first. If you treat him as if he is okay and say, "I'll be happy to take care of it however you want it," you break up his game. Nothing works on Dick like fulfilling his request promptly and accurately.

Stick with your game. When you can't break up Dick's game or bend the rules, you can still play in good faith. Accentuate the positive by repeating what you can do for him.

Freeloading Freda

A material girl in a material world, she wants her dollar's worth—and yours, and mine, and anyone else's she can get. She doesn't make a game of getting more for her money—for her, it's a war.

Sample Behaviors

Wants something for nothing—or better yet—two for nothing, brings something back when it wears out, breaks, or begins to bore her, and screams lawsuit or slander if accused of taking advantage.

Ways to Work with Freda

- *Treat Freda with the same courtesy and respect you would give to any customer.* You can show courtesy and deference without giving away the store.
- *Find a fair response to Freda's complaint (fair in your mind and in hers).*
- *You do not have to give in to Freda's demand.* However, giving in might be easier than avoiding the scene she's sure to cause with the other customers.

Look for the gifts—the things that every unpleasant encounter can teach you about dealing with ugly human behavior.

—Rebecca Morgan
Morgan Seminar Group

V

Knock Your Socks Off Service Fitness:

Taking Care of *You*

To this point we've focused our attention primarily on the customer. But there's another important player in the service game: *YOU!* A savvy service professional learns that self-management is every bit as important as managing the customer's experience.

Providing Knock Your Socks Off Service shouldn't be an impossible quest—or a personal ordeal. Like an athlete constantly in training, or a musician perfecting a performance, you need to develop, evaluate, pace, and care for yourself as well as your performance. That means work, but it also means celebrating a job well done.

How you feel about yourself and the job you are doing—whether you love it or are overwhelmed by it—will inevitably be reflected in the quality of your work. Knock Your Socks Off Service should be rewarding for everyone involved.

36

Master the Art of Calm

"The stress puzzle is the mind-body link: What roles do our emotions, thoughts, and perceptions play in the way we experience and physically respond to stressful situations?"

—Dr. Frances Meritt Stern
President, Institute of Behavioral Awareness

You're not any good to anyone when you are stressed out, overwrought, anxious, moody, belligerent, nasty, and still waiting for that first cup of coffee. The emotional labor involved in modern service jobs can actually be more draining than lifting boxes or pouring concrete. All the good stuff built into your job will never be enough if you don't learn how to cope with and counteract the stress.

In theme parks from Disneyland and Walt Disney World to Knott's Berry Farm, Universal Studios, and Six Flags, people at the front lines are taught the concepts of "onstage" and "offstage."

- *Onstage* is anywhere a customer can see or hear you.
- *Offstage* is everywhere else, safely away from the public eye.

An employee who is feeling stressed can ask a supervisor to take over the ride operation, concession stand, or broom so they can get themselves back together. Once offstage, they can let their emotions out, deal with them, put their game face back on, and come back to the job without worrying about their next customer getting the brunt of their frustration or irritation.

You, your manager, and your organization have to work together to manage the environment in which you work. But only you can manage the way you react to a given service encounter. How do you cope? There are any number of techniques for reducing stress, whether inside your cubicle or out on the sales floor. Find those that work best for you and practice them every day. Here are ten to get you started:

Ten Stress Reducers

1. *Breathe.* Deep breathing is one of the oldest and best stress-busting techniques. Stress can upset the normal balance of oxygen and carbon dioxide in your lungs. Deep breathing corrects this imbalance and can help you control panic thinking. Take a deep breath through your nose—hold it for seven seconds (no more)—then let it out slowly through your mouth. Do this three to six times.

2. *Smile.* You make your mood, and your mood can stress or relax you. Smiling is contagious. When you see a customer looking a little glum, make eye contact and turn on one of your best and brightest. Ninety-nine times out of a hundred, you'll get a smile right back.

3. *Laugh.* Maintaining a sense of humor is your best defense against stress. Stress psychologist Frances Meritt Stern tells of a difficult client she had been dealing with for years. "That clown is driving me up a wall!" she often complained. One day, she began to envision him complete with white-face, floppy shoes, and a wide, foolish grin. With this picture tickling her funny bone, she was able to manage her stress response and focus on doing her job.

4. *Let it out.* Keep your anger and frustration locked up inside and you are sure to show it on the outside. Instead, make an appointment with yourself to think about a particularly

stressful customer later—and then find a way to release the frustration in a private setting. Unacknowledged tension will eat you up, but delaying your reaction to stress-causing events can be constructive. It puts you in control.

> **TIP:** To get extra value from the technique, service representative Amy Gruber keeps a stress log of her most frustrating customers and situations. Adding an entry to the log helps calm her, and over several years the log has become a guide to dealing with her stress load.

5. *Take a one-minute vacation.* John Rondell, a sales consultant, creates a vivid image of himself snorkeling off a beautiful white-sand beach in the Caribbean. He has worked on the scene until he can transport himself there and lose all sense of time and place, even though his visits last only a minute or two. He often goes to his "favorite place" following a stressful call or before talking to a stress-inducing customer.

Go ahead. I'm in a State of Calm.

cBUSH

6. *Relax.* We tend to hold in tension by tightening our muscles. Instead, try isometrics: tensing and relaxing specific muscles or muscle groups. Make a fist, then relax it. Tighten your stomach muscles, then relax them. Push your palms against each other, then relax your arms. Some people get so good at it they can do their exercises right under the customer's nose.

7. *Do desk aerobics.* Exercise is a vital component of a stress-managed life. Try these two "desk-er-cizes":

- While sitting at your desk, raise your feet until your legs are almost parallel to the floor. Hold them there for three seconds, then let them down. Do this five times.
- Rotate your head forward and from side to side (but not back—that can strain rather than stretch). Roll your shoulders forward and then lift them up and back. This feels especially good after you've been sitting or standing for some time.

8. *Organize.* Organizing gives you a sense of control and lessens your stress level. "I organize the top of my desk whenever I am waiting on hold," says Eric Johnson, a telephone customer service representative. "Before I leave for the day, I make sure everything is put away, and that I have a list of priorities made out for the next day."

9. *Talk positive.* Vent your anger and frustration in positive ways. Sharing customer encounters with co-workers helps you find the humor in the situation and gain new ideas for handling similar situations. But constant negative talk that rehashes old ground will only re-create and reinforce, not diminish, your stress.

10. *Take a health break.* Change your normal breaks into stress breaks. Consider walking outside, reading a chapter from a favorite book, or just sitting with your eyes closed for a few minutes. Bring healthy snacks and juice to work to substitute for the standard coffee and candy bars.

To paraphrase: You only serve as good as you feel. You need to take care of yourself to take good care of your customers. And you are the only one who can.

"When your customer is the most anxious, you need to be at your best—most competent, confident, calmest, and in control of yourself."

—Chip R. Bell

37

Keep It Professional

"Every job is a self-portrait of the person who did it.
Autograph your work with excellence."

—From a poster in an auto repair shop

Today, it's common to hear executives and managers proclaim, "Customers are our best friends." But Knock Your Socks Off Service professionals know that, for all the light banter and personal fanfare, there's a critical difference between being friendly and having a friendship.

A friendly transaction is a clear and understandable goal in any business—treating customers courteously, attentively, and professionally mimics the "transactional treatment" we would give to a close personal friend (and, in doing so, greases the wheels of commerce).

A friendship, on the other hand, is a relationship that begins and continues outside the bounds of the workplace and involves personal commitments far beyond the scope of the normal customer/server interactions.

Does that mean that customers should never be friends, or that friends shouldn't be customers? Of course not. We all hope our friends will chose to do business with us, and it's not unusual—and typically quite a compliment—when business relationships grow into interesting friendships.

If the letters to advice columnists are to be believed, it seems that a good percentage of today's romantic relationships grow out of service professionals meeting customers. But that's the result of a relationship that continues off the job.

Taking Care of Business

On the job, your customers are customers first and foremost: They have come to you not for conversation and companionship, but because they are trying to get their needs met through the business that employs you. Your customers need your help as a service professional, be it to ring up a sale, create a new hairstyle, or respond to their e-mail in a timely fashion. They aren't there to look for a new friend.

> **TIP:** You are the most helpful when you remain professional, but with a personal touch. That means not confusing your off-the-job personal friendships with on-the-job, friendly, professional transactions.

It's worth noting that friendships can suffer some bruises when business gets in the way. Do your friends feel secure enough in your friendship to risk your displeasure if your business services aren't satisfying? Even friends of long standing may feel uncomfortable being honest with you in a business relationship that seems more a friendship than a professional partnership. They may withhold pointed feedback or suppress complaints and ultimately may even take their business elsewhere rather than create hurt feelings by telling you about their dissatisfaction.

Appearances also have an effect, both on customers who don't know you as well and on supervisors and co-workers who do.

The next person waiting in line may be made distinctly uncomfortable by the personal chatter and other evidences of a relationship that excludes them. Even though they may not be waiting any longer than normal, that wait will "feel"' longer to them if they think you could get to their needs more quickly by dispensing with what appears to them to be idle chitchat.

Your co-workers and managers may have a similar reaction if they think you're giving unequal or preferential treatment to one particular customer, especially if there are other customers nearby waiting and watching.

Remember that a Moment of Truth for you and your business involves any time your customer has an opportunity to observe what you do and make a judgment on the quality involved. The best rule of thumb is to "keep it professional" at all times.

Involvement Varies

The difference between friendly and friendship and the difference between empathy and sympathy are related. When your friends experience pain or joy, you share those feelings with them. In that context, you sympathize as part of your friendship. When friends are in trouble, you may even offer advice. But it is not your role to fix everything for them.

When customers are upset, they expect you to care, too. But they also expect you to do something else that has nothing to do with a personal relationship: fix their problem and make things right without becoming personally involved. Showing empathy as part of being "professionally friendly" is the best way to respect the difference between personal and professional conduct.

We conducted an informal poll of service professionals and customers, asking the question, "How can you tell that a

service provider is a professional? The most frequently given answers are listed in Table 37-1.

Table 37-1.

Professional	Unprofessional
• Looks the part; neatly dressed	• Ignores you; usually in favor of a pesonal call or chat with a co-worker
• Confident communicator; doesn't "uhm," and say "I don't know" without trying to find out	• Sighs a lot; rolls his or her eyes
• Smiles; looks eager to help	• Chews gum or eats while talking to you

Who You Are vs. What You Do

There's another personal relationship that often gets overlooked by service professionals caught up in the trials or tribulations of their own jobs: the one between you and those closest to you—your family and loved ones. When family members ask the question, "And how was your day?" there usually is no shortage of service stories you can share with them. But while those tales can help your family better understand why you care so much about the work you do, it's unfair to overburden them with your professional concerns, just as it's unprofessional to violate the confidences of your customers. Tell your loved ones about what you do on the job each day, but try to balance any bad stories or experiences with the good.

TIP: Draw a clear line between who you are and what you do — who you are goes home with you at the end of the day; what you do stays at work.

Good service is not smiling at the customer, but getting the customer to smile at you.

—Dr. Barrie Hopson and Mike Scally
12 Steps to Success Through Service

38

The Competence Principle:

Always Be Learning

"You're never off duty; you have to remember everything you see."

—Holly Stiel
Concierge, Hyatt San Francisco

You've seen them. Maybe you've even worn one. You know, those little tags that say "Trainee." The ones that proclaim to all the world, "Be patient, I'm still learning."

We often think of trainees as young, anxious to learn, full of questions—and as people who can't wait to take off the trainee label and finally know it all. But delivering Knock Your Socks Off Service means having a lifelong learning mentality. Learning your job doesn't stop when you turn in the Trainee tag. In fact, it's just beginning. Like professional athletes, the best customer service people are always in training, always looking for ways to improve their performance, always seeking ways to hone their service edge.

What do you need to know? Think of lifelong learning as a personal customer service workout program. Just as with any form of effective cross-training, your fitness regimen should cover several interrelated areas. There are five basics: technical skills, interpersonal skills, product and service knowledge, customer knowledge, and personal skills. All are going to be critical to your success.

Use the questions below to test your strengths and weaknesses. You may keep your answers confidential, so don't be afraid to be critical. At the same time, it's important to take credit for the many good and right things you already do.

Technical/Systems Skills

	No	Yes
1. I have the skills and training to use our telephone and communications technology.	☐	☐
2. I have the skills and training to use my computer, e-mail system, web site, social media, and other technology in my work.	☐	☐
3. I know how to use organization systems and procedures to serve my customers.	☐	☐
4. When I need assistance using our technology or systems, I seek it in a timely manner.	☐	☐
5. I understand and can complete the paperwork required from my customers, and from me.	☐	☐

Interpersonal Skills

	No	Yes
1. I know the behaviors and attitudes that lead customers to say, "You really knocked my socks off!"	☐	☐
2. I can use specific techniques to calm angry or frustrated customers.	☐	☐
3. I can empathize with my customer's perspective.	☐	☐
4. I have insight into my own personality style and how best to respond to the styles of others.	☐	☐
5. I develop a feeling of partnership with customers and co-workers.	☐	☐

Product and Service Knowledge

	No	Yes
1. I can explain how my area's products and services contribute to my organization's overall success.	☐	☐
2. I can compare our products and services with those offered by our competitors.	☐	☐
3. I have the information I need about new or planned products and service offerings.	☐	☐
4. I know the technical terms and jargon, but I can explain them in plain English.	☐	☐
5. I know the most frequently asked questions, and the answers.	☐	☐

Customer Knowledge

	No	Yes
1. I know what customers complain about, and what customers compliment us on.	☐	☐
2. I know why customers choose us over our competition.	☐	☐
3. I know the "profiles" of my five most important customers/customer groups.	☐	☐
4. I know how the service I provide impacts the way customers rate us on quality measures.	☐	☐
5. I continually look for new ways to provide Knock Your Socks Off Service.	☐	☐

Personal Skills

	No	Yes
1. I deal constructively with on-the-job stress.	☐	☐
2. I find new challenges and insights, even when doing "the same old thing" for customers.	☐	☐
3. I organize and prioritize so I get the right things done in the right order.	☐	☐
4. When faced with customer frustration or anger, I don't take it personally.	☐	☐
5. The work I am doing now provides an important step toward my long-term goals.	☐	☐

Learning Is Systematic

Keeping a "learning log," a notebook or electronic journal that's always accessible in which you write both questions and answers, will help you better define your learning goals and improve your service performance. Organize your efforts: You can't learn everything at once, so don't try. Focus your lifelong learning program on one area at a time.

Put Yourself in Training

Use the space below—or your Learning Log—to list five knowledge or skill areas that you would like to improve or add to your talent bank.

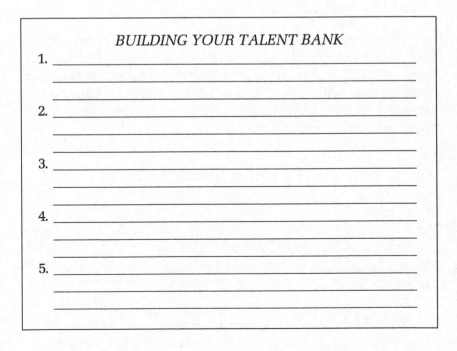

BUILDING YOUR TALENT BANK

1. _____

2. _____

3. _____

4. _____

5. _____

In the space below, identify two things you could do right now, without asking permission or investing a lot of money, to improve those skills. For example, you may want to ask a co-worker how she keeps her cool when customers burn red hot. Or you may ask to attend the next meeting of the local SO-CAP (Society of Consumer Affairs Professionals, Alexandria, Virginia), ICSA (International Customer Service Association, Chicago, Illinois), or Chamber of Commerce to hear a speaker on customer service skills.

TWO THINGS I CAN DO RIGHT NOW:

1.

2.

Now, identify two things that would require greater effort from you and cooperation from others. For example, you may want to enroll in a local college to earn a degree. Or you may want to meet with your manager to find out how you can become an internal expert on your area's computer systems or telephone technologies.

TWO THINGS TO EXPLORE FOR THE FUTURE:

1.

2.

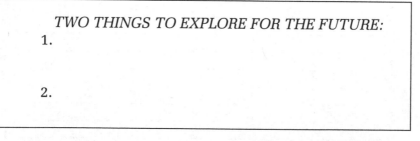

"Anyone who stops learning is old, whether at twenty or eighty. Anyone who keeps learning stays young. The greatest thing in life is to keep your mind young."

—Henry Ford

39

Party Hearty

"You deserve a break today!"

—McDonald's Jingle

It's true. You do deserve a break today—and every day! It's important to take time out to celebrate your successes. Be good to yourself for doing a terrific job. No one else can celebrate as well as you can because no one else knows how well you've done.

If you've ever spent an hour or ten complaining about stupid customers or unsolvable problems—and who hasn't—remember the rule of "equal time." Spend as much time, or better yet more time, rehashing your successes. From time to time go out with your colleagues and celebrate each other for surviving and thriving in the work you do. Is it bragging about yourself? Sure. But there's no reason to downplay your skills and accomplishments. And recognizing your successes today will help motivate you to come back for more tomorrow.

Learning to Celebrate

Some people seem born knowing how to give themselves, and the people around them, needed pats on the back for work well done. But for most of us, celebrating ourselves doesn't come easy. We get so embarrassed when others start to sing our praises we wouldn't even think of jumping in with a verse or two of our own. That's an attitude Knock Your Socks Off Service professionals can—and should—learn to leave behind. Give yourself permission to be terrific. That's right: You need to make a conscious decision to allow yourself to occasionally revel in doing well. Once you do, we guarantee you'll learn to love the habit.

Still think it will be hard to get the hang of this positive feedback thing? Then start by practicing on someone else. Thank a colleague for helping you out. Make a point of letting your supervisor know something good about a co-worker. Pass along a tip or trick you've learned from someone else—and make it clear who taught it to you.

Notice that these examples have a common element: They focus attention first on an action or accomplishment, then on the individual or team of individuals involved. In other words, you're not glowing all over someone just for being a wonderful person. Rather, you're taking note of what they did and why it was so terrific. Now start doing the same thing for yourself.

Five Ways to Celebrate

There are countless ways to observe and have fun with your service successes. But take some advice from Yertle the Turtle.

He tried to celebrate his own worth by rising high on the backs of his fellow turtles. It worked for a while, but eventually Yertle met the fate shared by all who lift themselves up by putting others down: He ended up doing a face-plant in the mud. Standing tall on the merits of your own service successes means celebrating personal victories, but it also means seeking out and celebrating the victories of your co-workers as well. Try these five ways to celebrate:

1. *Take yourself out to lunch.* Treat yourself to a special lunch or dinner or even breakfast. Invite a friend or co-worker (or several) to go along and—this is the important part—make sure they know exactly what you are celebrating and why.

2. *Take a co-worker out to lunch.* This one works the same as the one above, only this time the reason for celebration is a good service performance that has inspired you or given you added satisfaction or motivation in your job. Involving several

others reinforces the teamwork and camaraderie that makes good service organizations something special to be a part of.

3. *Buy balloons or flowers or something fun.* A balloon or fresh-cut flower on your desk can symbolize a recent service achievement. It also brightens up your work space and lets other people know you're feeling good about something. When they ask you, you'll have a chance to explain, which will make you feel even better.

> **TIP:** Consider giving the impromptu award you've presented yourself "legs:" Enjoy it on your desk for a day, then pass it on to a co-worker who just handled a Customer From Hell with grace and aplomb.

4. *Make a "brag sheet."* When you spend a lot of time working on the skills you'd like to improve, it's easy to forget to celebrate the strengths you already have. Start a list. When you have the inevitable bad day and are a little down in the dumps, pull out your brag sheet. It'll help put things in the proper perspective.

5. *Tell yourself, "You done good!"* Think talking to yourself is a little strange? It isn't. (Arguing with yourself, on the

other hand, is a little suspect.) Good news gets better in the telling. If you're not quite ready to shout it from the rooftops, at least tell yourself, verbally, with force and feeling, that you've done a good job.

> **TIP:** Be specific. Tell yourself exactly what you did well, better than you've ever done in the past. Or spread it around to co-workers: "I watched you with that customer. She asked some pretty tough questions, but you had all the answers and sent her out of here feeling great. Nice job."

"What gets rewarded gets repeated."

—Incentive and recognition axiom

Activities Connections

The activities listed here can be found in our book, *101 Activities for Delivering Knock Your Socks Off Service* (AMACOM, 2009). Incorporating these brief activities can provide great opportunities for learning, whether it be a brown bag lunch, an early morning staff meeting, or just a small group committed to improving their quality of service. We encourage you to check them out and give them a go!

Chapter 1: Activity #4, *Customers' Ever Changing Needs* (pp. 12–13). Consider both how expectations are changing and how different age customers want to experience service.

Chapter 3: Activity #7: *The Value of Reliability* (pp. 21–23). Look at organizations who deliver consistently reliable service versus those who do not.

Chapter 4: Activity #10: *The Language of Competence* (pp. 31–35). A game to sort and determine which words and phrases send a message of competence and create confidence on the part of customers.

Chapter 5: Activity #13: *Tangibles: Take a Field Trip* (pp. 41–44). Walk to the outside of your building and observe all the tangibles a customer sees before reaching your desk.

Chapter 7: Activity #22: *Responsiveness—Identifying the Barriers* (pp. 68–71). Consider what gets in the way of being Responsive at your organization.

Chapter 8: Activity #26: *The Customer is always. . .The Customer* (pp. 92–94). Consider the difference when you have been made to feel guilty by a service provider versus when you have been made to feel innocent first.

Chapter 10: Activity #31: *Making Exceptions* (pp. 109–112). Identify when making exceptions to rules is justified in the name of meeting customer needs.

Chapter 26: Activity #75: *Making "Thank You" Personal* (pp. 258–259). Create a thank-you format that works for everyone and plan how to incorporate it into daily interactions.

Chapter 27: Activity #78: *How Ready Are You To Recover?* (pp. 268–277). Take this assessment for individual and corporate readiness of the Recovery Process.

Chapter 28: Activity #82: *Tell Me a Story* (pp. 286–287). Learn from your own experience about what makes a positive, memorable recovery situation.

Chapter 29: Activity #79: *Using the Well-Placed "I'm Sorry"* (pp. 278–280). Identify when apologies are most often needed and plan how to say them.

Chapter 30: Activity #87: *Fix the Customer Role-Play* (pp. 303–305). Practice using the soothing words and phrases and skills for each color of upset customer.

Chapter 31: Activity #80: *Finding the Right Fix* (pp. 281–282). Identify common customer problems and agree on a range of options for resolving them.

Chapter 32: Activity #84: *Maximize Your Web Site Impact* (pp. 292–294). Build awareness of the customer's buying experience and the value of frontline "listening posts."

Chapter 33: Activity #81: *Putting Recovery Knowledge into Action* (pp. 283–285). Analyze a recent or current recovery situation via any medium and see how to improve the next time.

Chapter 34: Activity #88: *Calming Obnoxious Customers* (pp. 306–308). Master the steps in dealing with obnoxious customers and apply the techniques to real situations.

Chapter 36: Activity #93: *Create a Stress Log* (pp. 327–328). Familiarize yourself with the things that set you off in your service roles.

Chapter 37: Activity #97: *Keep it Professional* (pp. 340–342). Remember the importance of keeping all transactions professional.

Chapter 39: Activity #100: *For All You Do, This Note's For You* (pp. 350–352). Practice saying "thank you" for your own successes and accomplishments.

The "Knock Your Socks Off" Library

The following are all available from AMACOM Books:

Delivering Knock Your Socks Off Service
Managing Knock Your Socks Off Service: 2nd Edition
Sustaining Knock Your Socks Off Service
Knock Your Socks Off Answers
Knock Your Socks Off Coaching
Tales of Knock Your Socks Off Service (no longer in print)
Knock Your Socks Off Service Recovery
Knock Your Socks Off Selling
Knock Your Socks Off Prospecting
101 Activities for Delivering Knock Your Socks Off Service

Index

About Performance Research Associates, Inc.

Performance Research Associates, Inc.—founded in 1972 by the late Ron Zemke, one of the leaders of the American customer service revolution—trains and consults with organizations of all types and sizes on service quality, customer loyalty, and creating a customer-driven culture.

Performance Research Associates clients have included GlaxoSmithKline, First Union Corporation, Hartsfield-Jackson Atlanta International Airport, American Express Financial Advisors, PriceWaterhouseCoopers, Prudential Insurance, Harley-Davison, Dun & Bradstreet, CUNA, Roche Diagnostic Systems, Oppenheimer Funds, Microsoft, Broadbase Software, General Reinsurance, Motorola, Universal Studios Theme Parks, Deluxe Corporation, and Turner Broadcasting System.

The firm is headquartered in Minneapolis, Minnesota. For more information, please visit our web site: www.socksoff.com

About the Editors

Ann Thomas brings more than twenty years' experience in consulting and training to each of her clients. Her work has been focused in the areas of improving service quality, diversity awareness, generational differences, sales, performance management, and professional development.

As the sole licensed facilitator for Performance Research Associates since 1999, Ann's clients include Atlanta Hartsfield-Jackson International Airport; Depository Trust and Clearing Corporation; Marriott ExecuStay; The Mall of America; NuCompass Mobility Services; Turner Broadcasting; Advantage Health Systems; Accenture; The Securities Exchange Commission; Daimler Chrysler; Plexent; the Universities of Connecticut, Alabama, Iowa, Kansas, and Texas; Inter-American Development Bank; National Geospacial Agency; The Chicago Mercantile Exchange; and many others.

Ann does extensive volunteer work within her community. In her off hours, Ann enjoys working in her garden, walking, sailing, and spending time with her family.

Jill Applegate spent more than twenty years as project manager and client coordinator with Performance Research Associates, where she was also Ron Zemke's right hand. Jill takes seriously the responsibility of wowing customers on a daily basis.

She is currently working at U.S. Bank, where she continues to hone and share her Knock Your Socks Off Service skills with customers and co-workers alike.

Jill stays busy volunteering in her church, playing the piano, watching football, and taking frequent trips to Walt Disney World and other theme parks, and is proud of her up-to-date roller coaster resume.